A Brief History of British South Asian Art

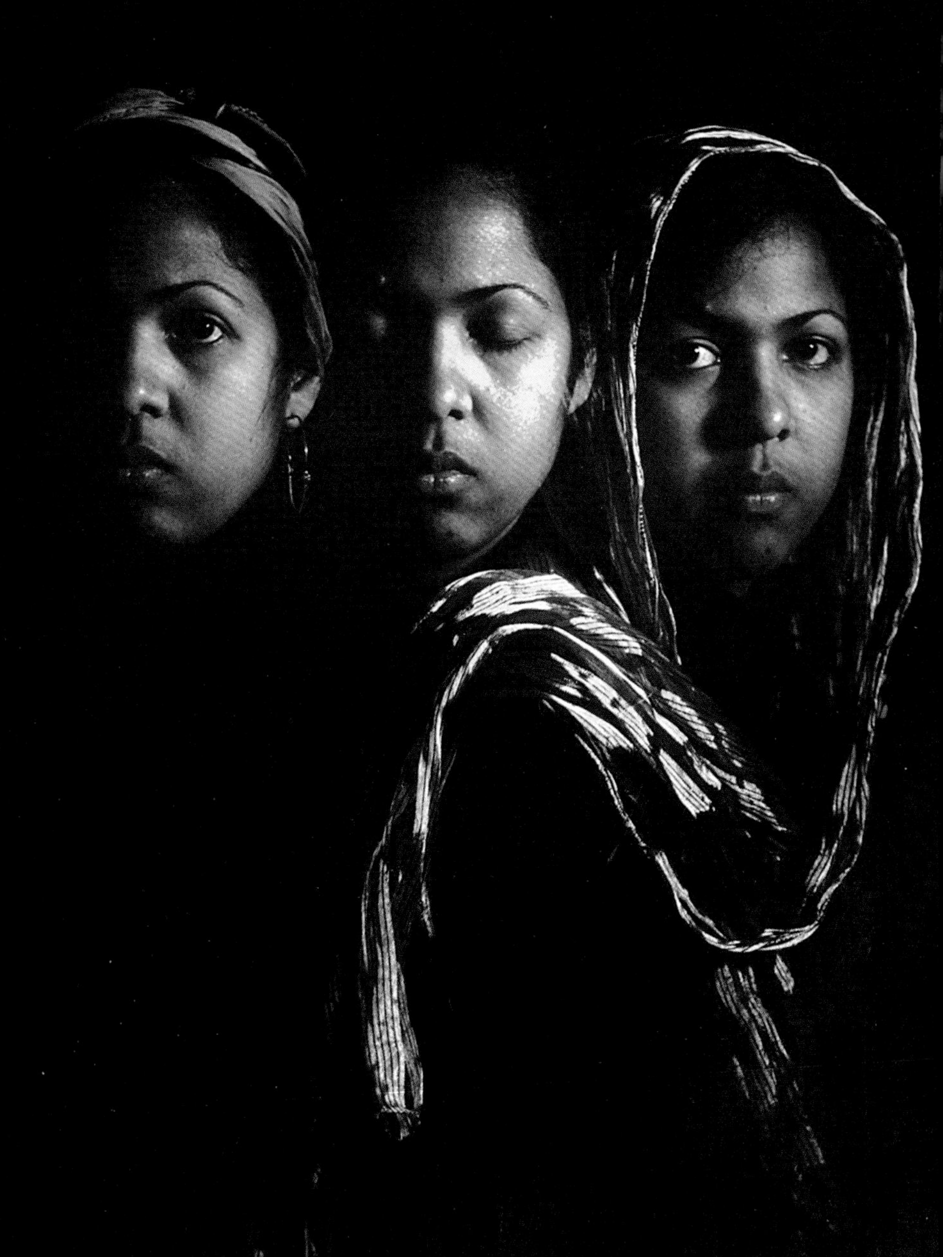

Alina Khakoo

A Brief History of British South Asian Art

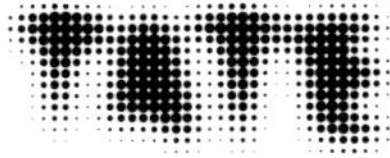

Commissioning Editor: Emma Poulter
Assistant Editor: Nicola Hands
Production: Roanne Marner
Picture Researcher: Deborah Metherell
Designed by Arati Devasher
Colour reproduction by DL Imaging Ltd.
Printed and bound in China by C&C Offset Printing Co., Ltd.

Front cover: Sutapa Biswas *Housewives with Steak-Knives*
1983-85 (detail, see p.59)
Back cover: Anwar Jalal Shemza *Meem Two* 1967 (detail,
see p.39)
Frontispiece: Roshini Kempadoo *Identity in Production*
1990 (detail, see p.101)

Measurements of artworks are given in centimetres, height
before width and depth

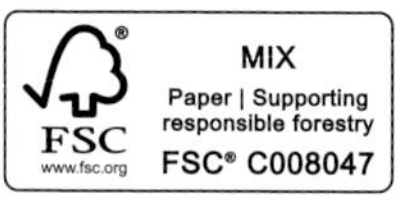

In solidarity with the artists, cultural workers and people
of Palestine.

Author Acknowledgements
Thank you to Emma Poulter, Nicola Hands, Arati Devasher,
Deborah Metherell and Tom Avery for steering this book
through twists and turns, and for ensuring such a polished,
scrupulously compiled and visually stunning end result.
Thank you to the numerous artists and artists' estates
who supported the reproduction of their artworks and
answered my questions; thank you especially to those who
welcomed me into their homes. For offering wisdom of
various kinds, thank you to Shreeya Makwana, Hammad
Nasar, Siddharth Soni, Imogen Cosgrave, Nicholas Brown,
Bhajan Hunjan, Janice Cheddie, Bethan Bide, Alistair O'Neill,
Shalmali Shetty, Simeran Gell, Helen Taylor, Lotte Crawford,
Harry Adams, Tom Chesworth, Shukla Sawant and Arushi
Vats. Thank you to Priyamvada Gopal, Amy Tobin and
Shamira A. Meghani for supervising the doctoral thesis
out of which this book has grown. Thank you to the many
librarians, archivists and staff of museums and galleries
who facilitated my research, especially the Cambridge
University Library Inter-Library Loans team. Thank you to
Kevin Greenbank for giving me the space in which much
of this book was written. Sarah Ali's advice, practical
support and cooking have been this book's sustenance.
Thank you most of all to Gulamabbas, Sabira and Iman
Khakoo, and Sakina Karim for their care, encouragement
and understanding. Love and thank you to David Ewing for
thinking through every idea in this book with me, and for
holding onto my dreams.

CONTENTS

7   Introduction: Two Waves of
Postwar British South Asian Art

22   The Works

150   Notes

156   Further Reading

157   Credits

158   Index

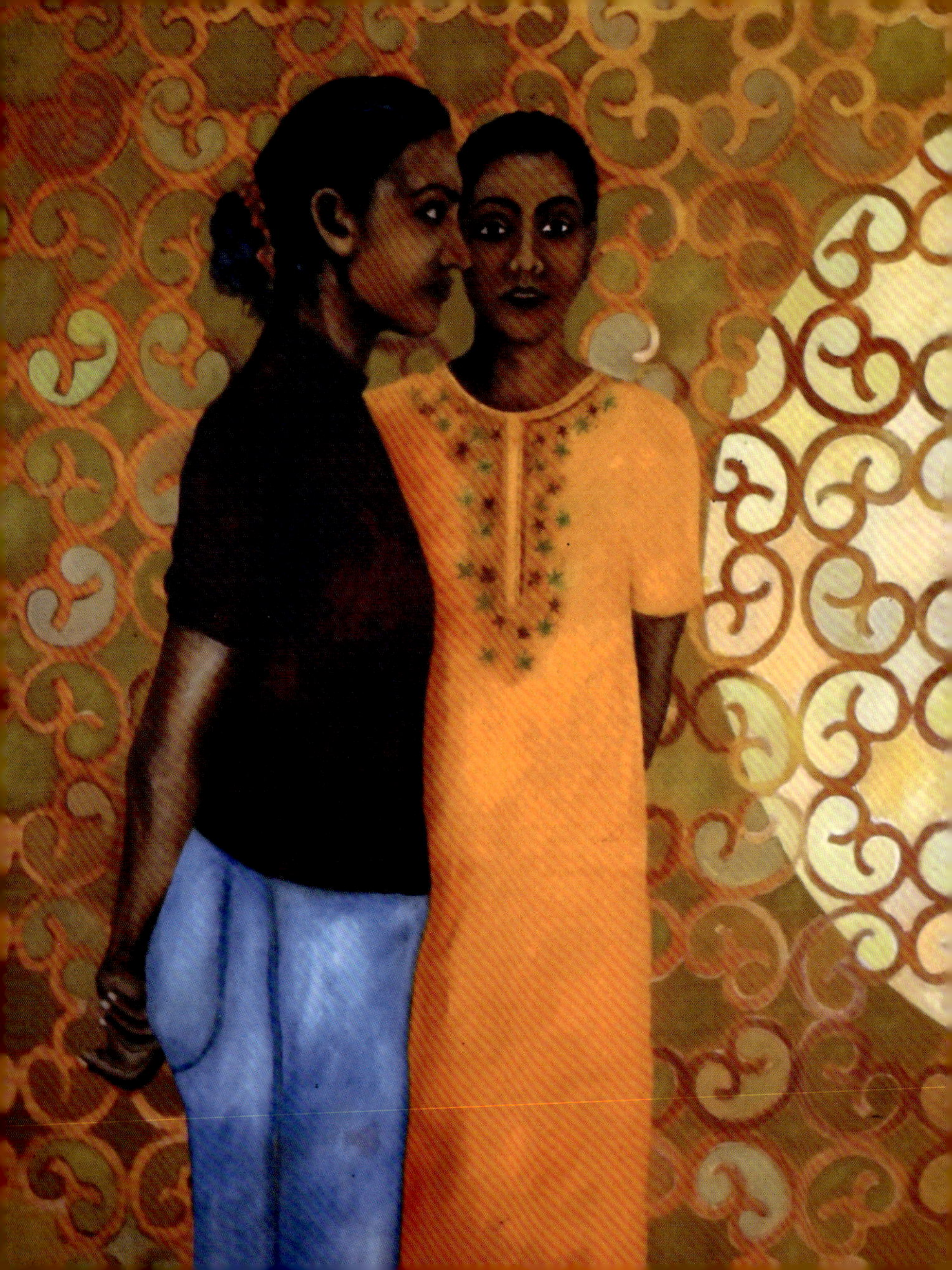

INTRODUCTION: TWO WAVES OF POSTWAR BRITISH SOUTH ASIAN ART

The narrator of *Emergence*, Pratibha Parmar's experimental film of 1986 (p.81), tells us that a circle of diasporic feminist artists is 'rising, rising, rising', from the rubble of the British Empire 'to tomorrow's dreams'. Scenes of England's landscape are overlaid with a cacophony of white noise. Other shots represent buildings on a dramatically slanted angle. What Parmar seems to be conveying to us, via visual and sonic metaphors, is that these artists, hailing from the former colonies and now living in the metropole, were transforming notions of Britain and Britishness.

Taking its lead from *Emergence* – while expanding Parmar's purview to encompass a range of art-historical constituencies from across the mid-to-late twentieth century – *A Brief History of British South Asian Art* affirms that artists connected to the subcontinent and its diaspora contributed to the production of Britishness 'from below'. It comprises concise readings of sixty-four artworks made between 1950 and 2002, which can be located in a purposefully relaxed understanding of 'British South Asian' socio-cultural geographies.[1] The book by no means covers the full span of British South Asian art, whose history dates back at least to the society portraits made by Poona-born Samuel Fyzee Rahamin (né Samuel Rahamin Samuel) while training at the Royal Academy, London, between 1903 and 1908, and continues into the present – not least with the award of the Turner Prize to Jasleen Kaur in 2024. However, this introduction will attempt to make the case for considering the period roughly spanning from decolonisation to the turn of the millennium as formative in the constitution of British South Asian art as we know it today.

Bhajan Hunjan *Dialogue II* 1993 (detail, see p.125)

In what follows, I will situate the sixty-four artworks in relation to two broad historical 'moments' or 'waves' mapped out in cultural theorist Stuart Hall's account of 'black' diaspora artists in postwar Britain: the first roughly spanning the years between 1945 and the mid-1970s, and the second running from the late 1970s to the turn of the millennium. In thinking about these contexts, it is helpful to bear in mind Hall's concept of the 'moment' or 'wave': terms he uses interchangeably to denote a set of 'striking convergences between very different kinds of work', as well as 'ideas, practices, social movements and political events' that might be assembled into a formation. The wave, in other words, provides an open-ended and historically specific way of thinking about the relationship between artworks, artists, and broader cultural, social and political realities. It is also important to note that Hall uses the term 'black' as it was used historically by anti-racist activists – that is, as a transcultural political identity, which structured alliances among people with roots in the formerly colonised world. As such, his account covers 'all the minority migrant communities' in postwar Britain.[2] This introduction, however, focuses on British South Asian constituencies, which in most respects fall within the purview of Hall's essay, but are not its major focus.

The First Wave: Cosmopolitan Modernists
Of the artists included in this book, the following participated in what we might designate as the first wave of postwar British South Asian art: Fatima Ahmed, Munira Al Kazi, Rasheed Araeen, Avinash Chandra, Prem Lata Chandra, Iqbal Geoffrey, Amal Ghosh, Balraj Khanna, Prafulla Mohanti, Ahmed Parvez, Ivan Peries, Lancelot Ribeiro, Anwar Jalal Shemza, F.N. Souza and Maria Souza. These artists were predominantly born in the 1920s and 1930s in various parts of the South Asian subcontinent, then under European colonial rule. They came from diverse backgrounds, but most were socio-economically privileged. Coming of age in the 1940s and 1950s, many first-wave artists were impacted by the seismic events

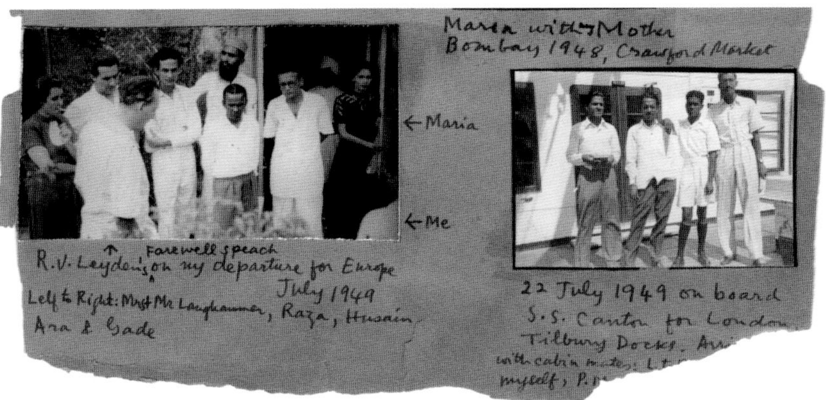

of the birth of new, independent South Asian nation-states, including
the extreme violence of partition from 1947 to 1948.[3] Many of them
attended art school, and launched their artistic careers, in this ambivalent
moment. As artists, it was through a modernist idiom that they felt able
to explore the violent upheavals and prospects for future progress that
decolonisation encompassed. As Hall elaborates, 'certainly, they continued
to paint and create with varying degrees of reference to the sights and
sounds, cultures and traditions, histories and memories of their places
of origin. However, increasingly they seemed to see these things within
a modern vision-field, via the modern consciousness of a certain "de-
territorialisation" of colour and form.'[4]

Participants in the first wave largely came to Britain in the 1950s,
arriving alongside artists from other parts of the decolonising world.
Some came for short periods, while others stayed indefinitely. Their
motivations for travelling were varied – some, as Hall describes, came 'to
fulfil their artistic ambitions and to participate in the heady atmosphere

F.N. Souza and others on board SS Canton for London, Tilbury Docks, 22 July 1949

of the most advanced centres of artistic innovation at that time . . . The
promise of decolonisation . . . liberated them from any lingering sense of
inferiority. Their aim was to engage the modern world as equals on its own
terrain.'[5] London was the destination for such artists. A photograph of F.N.
Souza and his shipmates on board the SS Canton bound for London in
1949, in which the artist (p.9, second from the left) slouches irreverently,
staring at the viewer as though making a wager, is a notably masculine
expression of this modern artistic, and postcolonial, sensibility. Another
motivating factor for artists' departures for Britain was dissatisfaction
with art scenes in South Asia. Art historian Karin Zitzewitz, for instance,
has described how 'F.N. Souza was pushed by his disgust for the art world
of Bombay. Souza was appalled by the response to his 1949 nude self-
portrait, which the police forced him to cover after complaints that it was
obscene.'[6] Others also came in search of various kinds of social freedoms.

When first-wave artists arrived in Britain, they found themselves
in a country still emerging from the rubble of the Second World War.
Attitudes towards foreigners could range from good-faith curiosity to
racist hostility, and vestiges of colonial culture remained. This set of
contexts influenced first-wave artists' lives in the former metropole. Many
of them were engaged in distinctly 'postwar' lines of artistic questioning;
for instance, art historian Rachel Garfield has argued that Avinash
Chandra's view of 'being an artist as a vocation with responsibilities' can be
understood as engaging discourses on 'mankind's omnipresence and the
humanistic belief in man's goodness' that were ascendant in the aftermath
of war.[7] For first-wave artists such as Chandra, London was a crucible
that transformed their practices. Others, however, had arrived in the city
with other vocations, and London's effect was to make them into artists.
Take, for example, Araeen's account of Khanna, who initially came to study
English literature: 'Confined to a small room in London, and with nothing
else to do, he began to doodle: . . . "I'm a naturally outgoing person and
to begin with it was very difficult, living in a small room. That feeling of

alienation' – which resonated with a broader social feeling these artists experienced as immigrants – 'can be devastating. Painting and drawing was one way of coping".[8]

Some artists came to thrive in the British art world, though rarely without a struggle for recognition. For instance, in 1962, Avinash Chandra became the subject of a BBC documentary, and in 1965 his painting *Hills of Gold* (p.35) became one of the first works by an artist born in South Asia to be collected by the Tate Gallery. Important platforms for first-wave artists were progressive independent galleries in London, notably Gallery One and the New Vision Centre. The Commonwealth Institute was also a site where first-wave artists could gain exposure, but only on the terms of the institution's geopolitical premise, which sat at odds with the agenda of decolonisation. In the 1960s, Maria Souza promoted the work of her then ex-husband, F.N. Souza, in her drawing room in the West End. From 1975 to 1985, she ran Arts 38, 'an international gallery for unestablished artists', from the same location.[9] Several first-wave artists made simultaneous contributions to other modern art worlds – for example, Al Kazi was committed to building a modern art culture in Kuwait. However, critical discussion of first-wave artists tended to exoticize them and to portray them as derivative of their Western counterparts.[10] Further, as Hall describes, while some artists secured acclaim, most found themselves barred from the art world, and ultimately found life in London a 'dispiriting affair'.[11]

In the face of this rejection, artists relied on kinship networks as informal sources of support and indeed inspiration. From the 1960s, first-wave artists also set up official collectives as part of a 'fight to promote ourselves' and to amass 'some kind of force', in the words of painter Yashwant Mali.[12] The first group of this kind was Pakistan Group London, which staged an exhibition of works by five artists from then East and West Pakistan at Woodstock Gallery, London in 1958. The second was the Indian Painters' Collective, formed in 1963 and pitched to Indian diplomats as a cultural bridge between India and the UK. This strategy garnered the group powerful connections and exhibition space in ambassadorial buildings; for instance, the collective organised an exhibition titled *Six Indian Painters* at India House in 1964. This group reconstituted itself twice during the 1970s and 1980s. The final group was the Indian Arts Council, active from 1985 to 1991, which traversed the first and second waves (as discussed below).[13] First-wave artists also agitated with artists from other parts of the formerly colonised world living in London; the short-lived Rainbow Art Group (founded in 1978), for instance, was a coalitional collective predominantly comprising artists from South Asia and the Caribbean.

The period from the 1960s to the 1970s also saw the flourishing of a more experimental artistic culture, invested in global emancipatory politics, including women's liberation, gay liberation, Third Worldism and Black Power. It was in this context that Araeen made *Fire!* (p.43), which he presented at a festival organised by the collective Artists for Democracy celebrating the US's defeat in Vietnam in 1975.

The Second Wave: Cyclonic Activity

Of the artists included in this book, the following contributed to the second wave of postwar British South Asian art: Said Adrus, Nudrat Afza, Nilofar Akmut, Ruhul Amin, Zarina Bhimji, Sutapa Biswas, the Black Audio Film Collective, Chila Kumari Singh Burman, Hamad Butt, Gurinder Chadha, Mohini Chandra, Jai Chuhan, Jamil Dehlavi, Poulomi Desai, Al-An deSouza, Nina Edge, Sunil Gupta, Mumtaz Karimjee, Permindar Kaur, Roshini Kempadoo, Keith Khan, Shakila Taranum Maan, Anita J. McKenzie, Shaheen Merali, Sarbjit Natt, Pratibha Parmar, Symrath Patti, Samena Rana, Alistair Raphael, Ian Iqbal Rashid, Retake Film and Video Collective, Parminder Sekhon, Fahmida Shah, Molly Shinhat, Gurminder Sikand, Veena Stephenson, Shafique Uddin, Yugesh Walia, Ali Mehdi Zaidi, and the members of the Mount Pleasant Photography Workshop.

These artists were for the most part born in the 1950s and 1960s, of various social backgrounds, including diverse migratory histories. Some, for instance, were second-generation immigrants born in Britain, whose parents had been part of the Windrush Generation – arriving from the Caribbean to fill postwar labour shortages – or had migrated from Punjab to Britain after partition. Others were first-generation immigrants, including a contingent that had been born into a middle class of South Asian colonial administrators and traders in East Africa, and who were forcibly expelled or felt compelled to leave from the late 1960s onwards after the instatement of policies aimed at redistributing power to the Black-majority population in newly independent nations. Others still formed part of a wave of arrivals from Bangladesh in the 1970s and 1980s in the wake of the Liberation War. Where most of the first wave came to Britain as artists, much of the second wave arrived via economic and political flows of migration quite separate from their artistic careers. As a consequence, the story of the second wave is not one that centres on London, but spans farther reaches of mainland Britain, from Bradford to Southampton.

What unified the second wave was participation in a powerful grassroots mobilisation against racism, which emerged in Britain in the 1970s and continued into the 1990s. This was a moment when the state galvanised public anxiety about immigrants' criminality and other forms of aberration, in order to secure popular consent for authoritarian politics, by which it sought to tackle a deepening economic crisis and heightened class conflict – as was famously argued at the time by cultural studies scholars.[14] While antagonising this set of socio-political forces, second-wave artists produced a spectrum of politicised art, drawing on the influences of leftist cultural theory and practice that was taught at some of their art schools, and circulated in printed forms. Their work ranged from reclamations of British South Asian cultural identities – denigrated as passive or exotic in public culture – to highly experimental disruptions of the notion of a stable cultural identity per se. Some artists even put

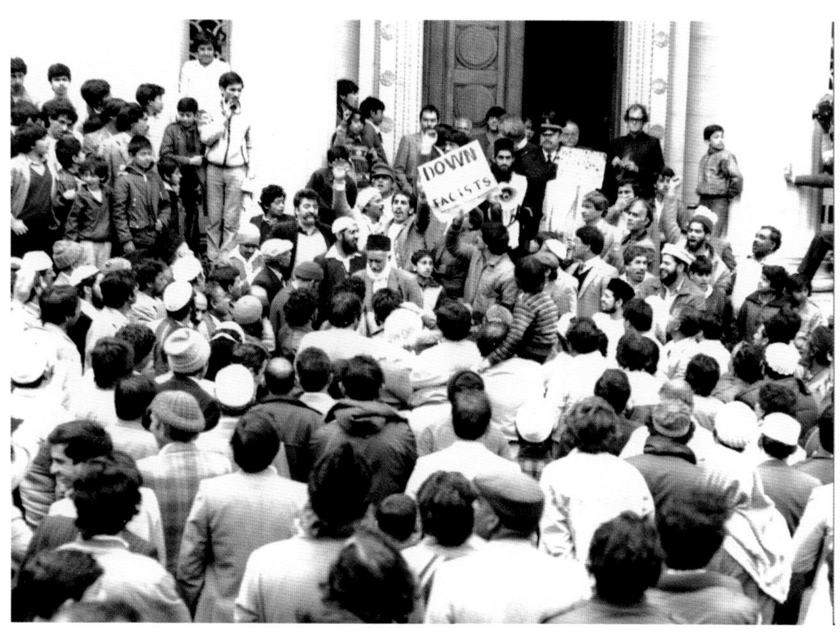

their work in the service of political campaigning; for example, Fahim
Qureshi photographed a sit-in outside Luton Town Hall after a pig's head
had been left outside Luton Mosque in 1981. This work not only fulfils the
vital task of documenting the protest, but also emphasises the agency of
the protestors: Qureshi's careful framing makes it seem as though the
crowd is expanding infinitely outwards. He also draws the viewer's eye to
a placard at the centre of the composition that bears the protest's key
message: 'DOWN [WITH THE] FASCISTS'.

Fahim Qureshi *Picket outside Luton Town Hall in protest
against a racist attack on Luton Mosque, which led to the
establishment of Luton Youth Movement* 1981

The anti-racist mobilisation of which the second wave formed part
was not straightforwardly unified. Instead, in Biswas's memorable phrase,
it was 'like cyclonic weather', comprising loosely connected zones of
intense energy, each with its own cultural, social and political set of
priorities, and its own forms of activity.[15] Each artist tactically chose
where to place their centre of gravity, often altering commitments
over time, as well as contributing to multiple sites at once. DeSouza's
practice, which spanned squatters' rights, Xerox art, Third Worldist art
and more, is exemplary of this provisionality and simultaneity. Among the
major sites of activity that formed part of this 'cyclonic weather' were a
transcultural 'black' arts culture, and transcultural 'black' feminist art. The
latter included the Blackwomen's Creativity Project founded by Maud
Sulter and Ingrid Pollard in 1982, out of which emerged the anthology
Passion: Discourses on Blackwomen's Creativity – which featured Edge's
Snakes and Ladders (p.73) on the cover. Others still were focused on
British South Asian feminist concerns, such as the public constituted
by *Mukti* magazine, where Bhimji published a version of *She Loved to
Breathe – Pure Silence* (p.85). Further formations that were part of the
metaphorical 'cyclonic activity' were queer South Asian spaces, such as
the sexual health organisation Naz, with which Sekhon has been involved
since the mid-1990s. Rana pioneered anti-racist, feminist, disability arts
activism, including by leading multiple institutional accessibility campaigns.
Participants in the broader network of left social movements of the
time, who undertook acts of anti-racist solidarity – such as Judy Harrison
of the Mount Pleasant Photography Workshop (p.45) – also made vital
contributions. Though constitutive of British South Asian social life,
caste does not appear to have been high on the agenda of any of the
zones; one important exception is Sunandan and Yugesh Walia's 1987
documentary film *Shadows of Caste*, which explores caste oppression
and anti-caste activism in Britain. Finally, deSouza's recent recollection
that they were rejecting gender conformity in their work, but that 'we

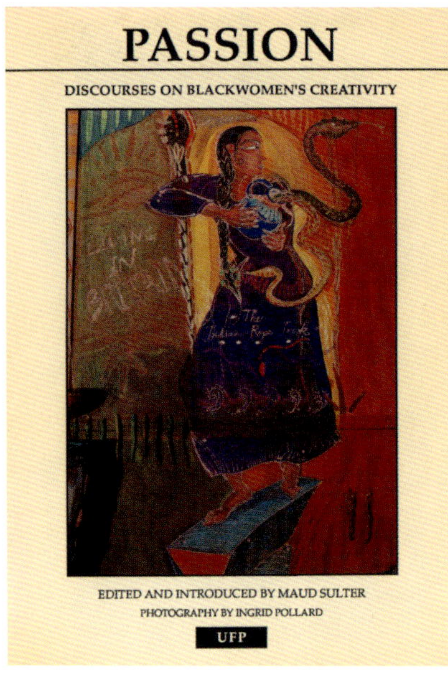

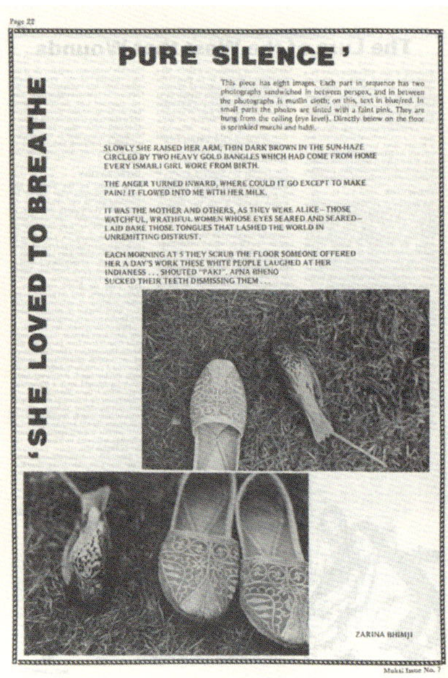

Page 22

PURE SILENCE '

'SHE LOVED TO BREATHE

This piece has eight images. Each part in sequence has two photographs sandwiched in between perspex, and in between the photographs is muslin cloth; on this, text in blue/red. In small parts the photos are tinted with a faint pink. They are hung from the ceiling (eye level). Directly below on the floor is sprinkled murchi and haldi.

SLOWLY SHE RAISED HER ARM, THIN DARK BROWN IN THE SUN-HAZE CIRCLED BY TWO HEAVY GOLD BANGLES WHICH HAD COME FROM HOME EVERY ISMAILI GIRL WORE FROM BIRTH.

THE ANGER TURNED INWARD, WHERE COULD IT GO EXCEPT TO MAKE PAIN? IT FLOWED INTO ME WITH HER MILK.

IT WAS THE MOTHER AND OTHERS, AS THEY WERE ALIKE—THOSE WATCHFUL, WRATHFUL WOMEN WHOSE EYES SEARED AND SEARED— I AID BARE THOSE TONGUES THAT LASHED THE WORLD IN UNREMITTING DISTRUST.

EACH MORNING AT 5 THEY SCRUB THE FLOOR SOMEONE OFFERED HER A DAY'S WORK THESE WHITE PEOPLE LAUGHED AT HER INDIANESS . . . SHOUTED "PAKI", APNA BHENO SUCKED THEIR TEETH DISMISSING THEM . . .

ZARINA BHIMJI

Mukti Issue No. 7

didn't have a language for it at the time', indicates that gender fluidity was being interrogated, yet not in a formalised mode, within this nexus of movements.[16]

The second wave was strongly committed to internationalism, in ways that contested the contemporaneous consolidation of national boundaries in the aftermath of decolonisation. Several artists formed part of a transatlantic South Asian diasporic culture of resistance. Rashid, for one, came over from Toronto in search of a more galvanising artistic

---

(left) *Passion: Discourses on Blackwomen's Creativity* 1990
(right) Zarina Bhimji's *She Loved to Breathe – Pure Silence* as featured in *Mukti,* no.7, 1987

environment than he could find at home: in his words, 'the South Asian community in London was ahead, and I needed to catch up with it.'[17]

The second wave sustained an ambivalent relation to the liberal multiculturalism espoused by state institutions – one which envisioned a society of intrinsically different communities coexisting harmoniously. Pivotal for the development of liberal-multicultural arts policy was the journalist and policymaker Naseem Khan's report *The Arts Britain Ignores* (1976), which called for a stream of funding to be dedicated to the arts practices of 'ethnic minority' communities. The politics of such policies, which aimed at forming a 'potential bridge' between cultures, as well as providing 'sustenance' to the communities themselves, were at odds with the revolutionary vision of social transformation espoused by most of the second wave.[18] Nevertheless, artists used them to draw crucial support for their work. This included making use of opportunities for commissions, acquisitions, residencies, teaching and funding in various kinds of public institutions. Second-wave cultural workers played significant roles in facilitating this patronage. However, many second-wave artists found their work constrained when forced to conform to the terms of liberal multiculturalism. One example is the Horizon Gallery, an independent gallery in Bloomsbury, west London, run by the aforementioned Indian Arts Council from 1987 to 1991. Horizon bridged the two waves, as it was primarily run by first-wave artists but provided many second-wave artists with their first solo exhibition opportunities. It was founded to realise the first wave's 'universalist and cosmopolitan' social and artistic vision.[19] In his speech at the gallery's launch party, Khanna proclaimed, 'Although our focus will necessarily be largely on work by South Asian artists, it is not our intention to limit selection to them. We intend to include artists from Britain, Europe and the Americas, from Africa and other parts of Asia, because our endeavour will be to provide a balanced view of the development of art generally, its world perspective.'[20] Yet, this was severely hampered by their state multiculturalist sponsors, who pressured them to

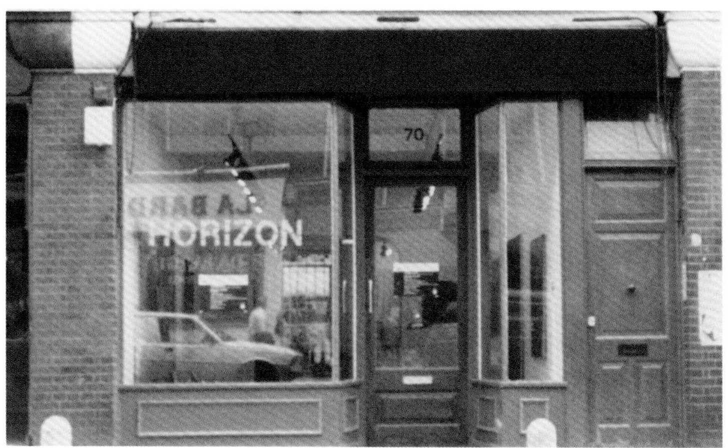

exhibit only artists of the British South Asian diaspora.

A number of the artistic practices discussed in this book do not sit easily in the structure of the two waves. Araeen is often cited as a transitional figure, yet Prodeepta Das, Avtarjeet Dhanjal, Sardul Gill, Bhajan Hunjan, Juginder Lamba, Shanti Panchal, Saleem Arif Quadri, Nadir Tharani and Shanti Thomas might also be seen as such. All were born roughly between the 1940s and mid-1950s, and most spent their early life in South Asia or East Africa. Most came to Britain as students in the 1960s and 1970s. Their work lies on a spectrum from the universalist tenets of the first wave to the political aesthetics of the second wave, often operating transversally across the two. The difficulty of categorising these artists' practices is a welcome obstruction from the ossification of the waves, and a salutary reminder that lived realities always exceed historical accounts.

First- and second-wave artists, along with their intermediaries, formed essential parts of the history of postwar British art, as well as having

Façade of Horizon Gallery, London, 1987

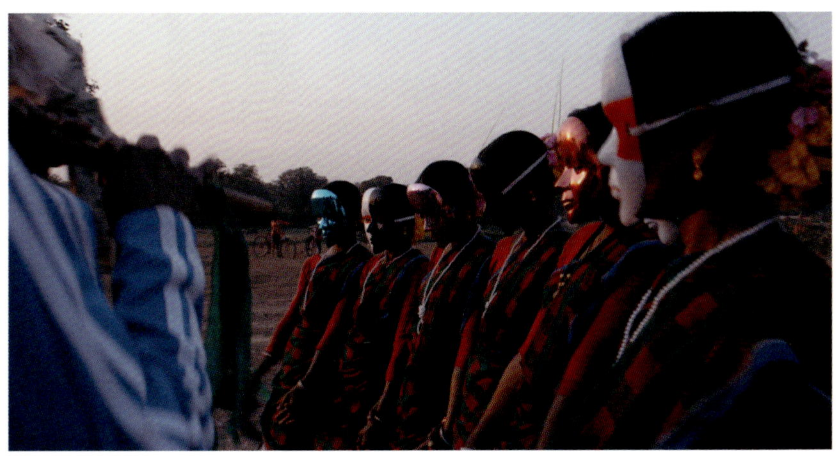

the broader effect of "'unwriting" … "our island story'", to quote Hall.[21] Their contributions were certainly made in the form of their artworks, but they also exceeded the making of art. For instance, Gill was a committed art educator in Nottingham for thirty years. In 1987, Khanna spearheaded a campaign for the V&A's Indian Collection to undergo a postcolonial reckoning, long before cultural decolonisation debates were at the fore of public discussion. Much of the diversity of representation now present in public cultural institutions has its origins in the second wave's dogged institutional activism. Their works also constitute rich source material for younger generations of contemporary artists. The Otolith Group, for instance, has engaged deeply with the work of the Black Audio Film Collective to produce its body of experimental films on fragmentary, international leftist archives – for instance, *O Horizon* 2018 on Rabindranath Tagore's anti-colonial environmental pedagogy enacted at Santiniketan, India. Many of the artists discussed in this book continue

The Otolith Group *O Horizon* 2018 HD Video 81 min 15 sec

to practice in contemporary 'moments' themselves – a further reminder
of the provisionality of the 'two waves' heuristic.

A Brief History of British South Asian Art: Overview

The remainder of this book comprises close readings of sixty-four
artworks that were 'constitutive elements' of the two waves of postwar
British South Asian art described above.[22] It aligns itself with a collective
endeavour by artists, art historians and curators to overturn amnesia
about the contributions of diasporic artists in postwar Britain. A crucial
part of this joint endeavour is to foreground artworks, and thereby
to resist a tendency to overemphasise diasporic artists' biographical
identities.[23] This book seeks to contribute to the building of a corpus of
visual analyses of artworks by diasporic artists in postwar Britain, primarily
by drawing out some of the socio-cultural particularities of British South
Asian constituencies. I offer new perspectives on relatively familiar works,
as well as highlighting and interpreting lesser-known works. My approach
to interpreting the artworks broadly follows Hall, who thinks of each
wave in discursive terms as a 'problem space' – using postcolonial theorist
David Scott's terminology. A problem space comprises 'a set of cognitive,
political [and artistic] questions which together create a "horizon"
of possible futures within which we "think the present"', to which art
practices can be read as constituting a reply.[24]

   It would be impossible to comprehensively represent all the artists
who contributed to the two waves. My selection includes works that
have sparked my interest and excitement, and which, taken together,
convey the diversity of postwar British South Asian art. This includes a
range of forms, from traditional fine-art mediums to film, photography,
fashion, textiles, ceramics and architecture. The first-wave artists
represented emerged in modern art movements in varied regions of
South Asia, and I have ensured a strong representation of women;
meanwhile, the second-wave artists included display a variety of

diasporic trajectories, and of single/plural heritages, as well as engaging in a wide span of 'zones' of cultural political activity. Where possible, I have selected works from public collections, so that readers can view them in person.[25] The politics of history – of which artists have their work recorded, collected and photographed – placed certain conditions on what this book could be. Notably, very little is currently known about first-wave artists who were women. This may be in part due to gendered conditions on their practice that caused disruptions – for instance, where women sacrificed their artistic careers to support those of their husbands. They have no doubt also faced the compounded deletions of women and diasporic artists from the record of postwar British art. In *A Brief History of British South Asian Art*, works by artists that do not fit perfectly within the book's scope, or reproductions of slides representing artworks that no longer survive, serve as reminders of the need for flexible art-historical practices that are able to represent the full breadth of marginalised histories, and indeed as invitations to action within and beyond the institutions of art history.[26]

Prem Lata Chandra 1931–75
Untitled c.1950s

Prem Lata Chandra's painting depicts a tree-like form, with the foliage comprising four intersecting heads, consisting of primary colours and thick outlines. Black-and-white striations create a kind of webbing around this figure. The work was likely produced at some point between the artist's enrolment at the Delhi Polytechnic art department in 1947, and the work's accession into the collection of the Government Museum and Art Gallery, Chandigarh, in 1962 (including following the artist's receipt of a scholarship to study in London, and her relocation to the city in 1955). Chandra's tutors at the Polytechnic were known for their investments in international modernism and socialist politics, and, eventually, for their proximity to the Indian government. Indeed, it is difficult to miss this work's engagement with various international modernist tendencies, including geometric abstraction; expressive layering and scraping of paint; and primitivist appropriations of African masks and children's drawings. At the same time, Chandra's form evokes various symbols of 'Indianness' in the contemporary nationalist imagination: it resembles a tree (a powerful symbol recalling Buddha's enlightenment, the guru under the tree, as well as constituting a synecdoche of the Indian village, perceived as the cradle of authentic Indian culture), with lines pulling it into a unitary form and drawing it into relation with the earth. The same form might also be interpreted as part of a charkha or spinning wheel (a symbol of India's autonomy from British industrial cotton), with the black-and-white webbing representing the spinning thread. Though it has often been neglected, Chandra's work is among the most powerful aesthetic articulations of the existential question facing the new Indian nation: 'how to recognise one's "Indianness" and be modern at the same time.'[1]

———————————

Oil paint on canvas
83.8 x 58.4

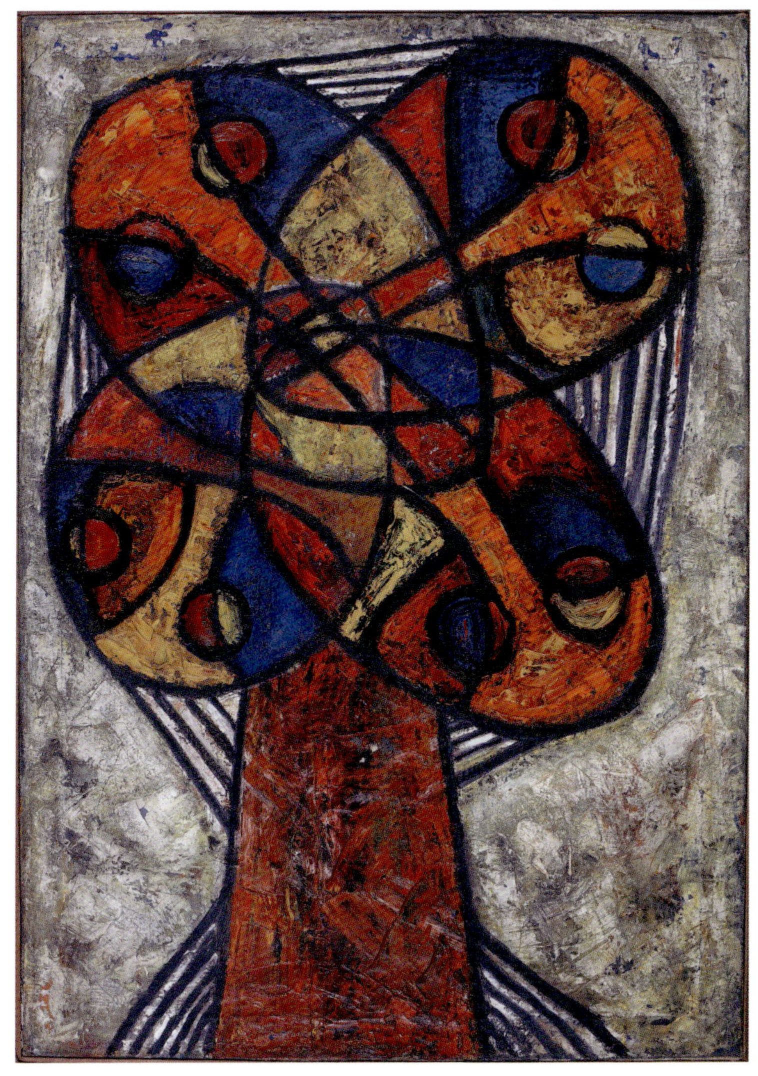

Iqbal Geoffrey 1939–2021
Epitaph 1958

Iqbal Geoffrey was an artist, art world activist, art educator, lawyer and accountant, distinctive for his eccentric persona. Born in Chiniot, India (now in Pakistan), in 1939, he was intent on succeeding in the West, and lived peripatetically between Britain, the US and Pakistan for much of his life. As art historian Gemma Sharpe suggests, the different parts of Geoffrey's career can all be understood within the rubric of his coinage of 'aesthETHICS', representing 'a commitment to truth and justice at all costs . . . in art, life and law'.[2] This often consisted of challenging what Geoffrey called 'technical truths', or Western pseudo-universalisms. Alongside his negotiation of postcolonial realities and universalist ideals in his art-institutional activism and legal work, Geoffrey's artworks provided a space for the artist to imagine new worlds structured by his values. *Epitaph* is one such work, even if it speaks in the first instance to the Pakistani politics of its time. It is a small painting comprising dense layers depicting a balanced configuration of three large geometric forms, and small details including outlined circles and slashes. Geoffrey has made the painting appear weathered, and the forms as though baked in, conveying a sense of primordial age. Meanwhile, the forms draw influence from ancient Indus Valley clay seals, and mandalas, as well as from art informel. In a letter dated 1962, Geoffrey wrote that the work – made in Montgomery, Pakistan – was an '*Epitaph* on 1958': the year that Field Marshal Ayub Khan staged a coup, and intensified existing authoritarianism.[3] As well as constituting an 'epitaph', the work also seems to advance an alternative cultural political vision, one that negotiates tradition and modernity, the local and the global, and the particular and universal: where South Asia's deep heritage meets a melding of trans-cultural references to create a transcendental aesthetic experience.

Oil paint, enamel paint, epoxy resin, charcoal and bronze powder on board
25.7 x 38.1

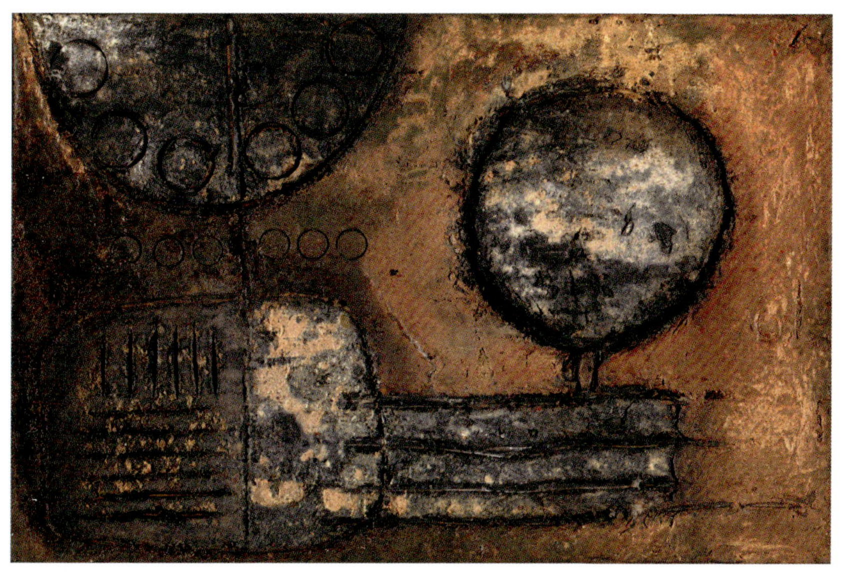

F.N. Souza 1924–2002
Crucifixion 1959

F.N. Souza moved to London from Bombay (now Mumbai) in 1949, driven
by a perception that it was 'the most cultured city in the world'.[4] At first
renting digs for foreign students while cleaning toilets to support his artistic
practice, Souza was soon joined by his first wife, Maria, who took on the
responsibility of financially supporting him, and who promoted his work
at her gallery Arts 38. In 1954, Souza sent an autobiographical essay titled
'Nirvana of a Maggot' to writer Stephen Spender, whose prompt support for
Souza helped bring on a wave of exposure and acclaim for his writing and
artwork. *Crucifixion* was painted in London in the wake of white nationalist
rioting in 1958, and in the same year as the racist murder of Antiguan-born
carpenter and prospective law student Kelso Cochrane, which was followed
by powerful anti-racist mobilisation. In short, the routine discrimination
experienced by people of colour – including the network of international
modernists in London to which Souza belonged – exploded with rage into
the public domain. This depiction of a crucified, Black Christ, with a blank
stare, no cross to support him, and bat wings and sprouting branches
that designate a status between human and non-human, is, to quote art
historian Gregory Salter, a representation of 'a moment of empty catharsis'
paralleling the riots. At the same time, by portraying a 'figure that has given
himself up to religion but who retains little redemptive connotations of a
typical crucifixion', Souza rebukes the Catholicism used as a colonial tool
in Portuguese Goa, where he was born in 1924.[5] In sum, *Crucifixion* draws
trans-local and trans-temporal connections between contemporary race
politics in Britain and global histories of colonialism.

Oil paint on board

183.1 x 122

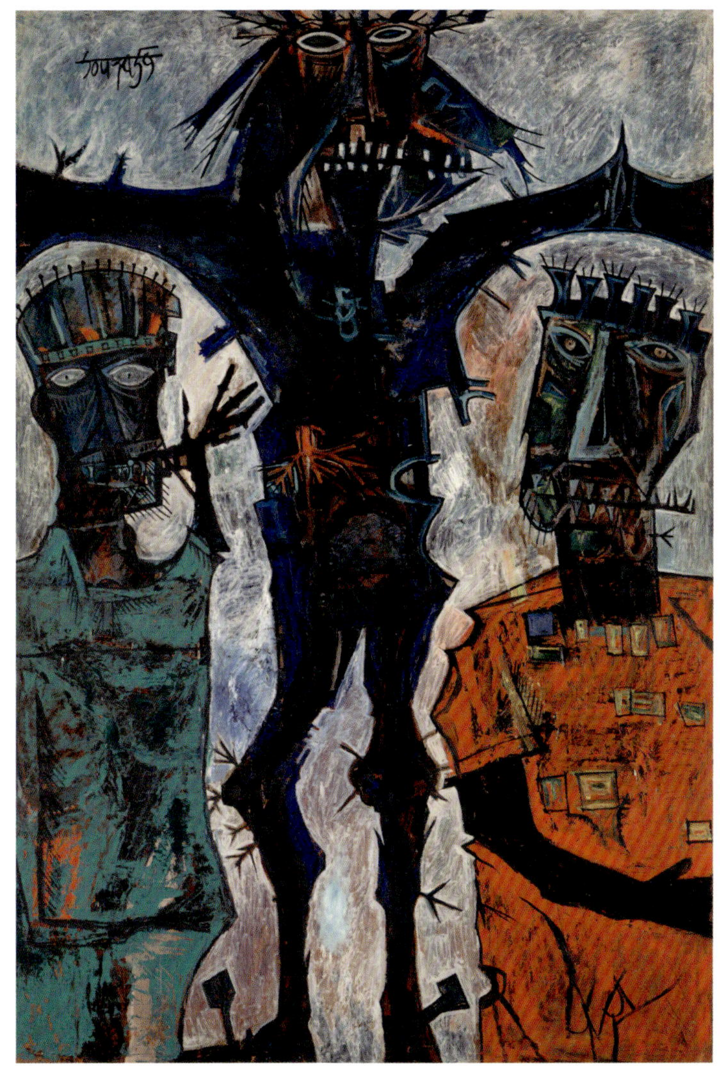

Prafulla Mohanti b.1936
Composition c.1962–4

Prafulla Mohanti is a key participant in neo-tantrism: an artistic movement that emerged in the 1960s among modernists in South Asia and the diaspora, which draws inspiration from the spiritual practice of tantra. Practitioners of tantra understand the universe as 'the concrete manifestation of the divine energy of the godhead', which they seek to channel through the human body and its energies.[6] Of the three main aspects of tantric philosophy, Mohanti's *Composition* relates to yantra, or the creation of markings and patterns to act as an aid to invoke the deity. The large, rotund forms could be interpreted as the bindu (cosmic dot), while a border of markings evokes the repetitive incantation of the 0 and 1, representing femininity and masculinity respectively; according to tantric philosophy, this binary must be transcended to attain oneness. The other patterns resemble rangoli designs, which represent mandalas, serving as a tool for devotees to invoke energies through visual and auditory chants, offering them protection. Equally important to Mohanti is that traditions such as rangoli are practiced locally in his birthplace, the village of Nanpur, Odisha. They provide metonyms for the villagers' principles of love, hospitality, and embedding art and spirituality in everyday life.[7] Mohanti's turn to neo-tantrism – one rooted in village culture – was linked to a critique of capitalism and racism, as manifested across South Asia and Britain. It followed his observation of industrial modernisation programmes that were disintegrating Nanpur's social structure. It also came in the wake of his encounter with social inequality in contemporary Britain, including class deprivation – such as he was exposed to while training as a town planner in Leeds at the time of making *Composition* – and racism, which he experienced personally.[8] Mohanti's neo-tantric, vernacular practice, of which *Composition* formed part, enabled the artist to advance an alternative value system to that of post-imperial, capitalist modernity, which he witnessed at several of its sharp ends.

Watercolour and body colour on paper

57 × 72.5

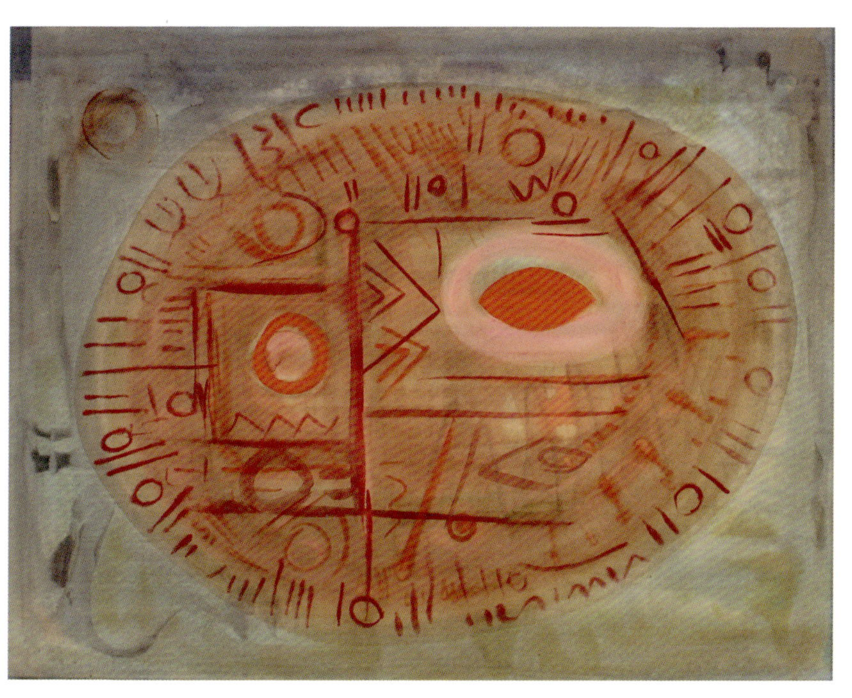

Munira Al Kazi 1939–2023
Mother 1963

In his introduction to Munira Al Kazi's 1964 exhibition at the New Vision Centre,
London, the artist and gallerist Denis Bowen wrote of Al Kazi's 'inspired personal
symbolism'.[9] In *Mother*, this symbolism consists of a downwards-pointing arrow,
touching the tip of a triangle to form an infinity sign. Within the arrow are two orbs,
one white and one black. Following a work produced the same year titled *Al-Qamar
Al Aswad*, these can be read as representations of the moon (an Islamic symbol of
cyclical transformation) and of the Black Stone (a relic now set within the Kaaba
in Mecca, understood as having fallen with Adam from Paradise, and having turned
black by absorbing worshippers' sins). The arrow intersects two rounded forms,
while the triangle pushes against the edge of a larger form from within. This imagery
resonates with motherhood, as well as with the many historical realities for which
mothers are tasked with providing metaphors. The three outlined forms, for instance,
might be read as a figurative representation of a mother's body as viewed by a child
lifted into the air – evoking the myopic intimacy of mother-infant relationships. At the
same time, the work's context of the mid-1960s prompts reflection on the relation
between its imagery and the use of maternal metaphors in the construction of anti-
colonial national imaginaries – one early example being 'Mother India'. What is more,
Stuart Hall reminds us that maternal metaphors were pertinent to the context of
ex-colonial arrivals (Al Kazi included) in Britain during the 1950s and 1960s. We might
connect their confrontation of Britain as both the 'mother country' and 'the mother
of all their troubles' with Al Kazi's representation of the moon and Black Stone, which
evoke themes of retribution and transformation.[10] With a symbolic schema relating
to notions of space, temporality, division and flux, *Mother* touches on questions that
loomed large at the end of empire, without abstracting the embodied mother who
was the basis of some of its most compelling metaphors.

Drypoint and mezzotint on paper
45.5 x 42.6

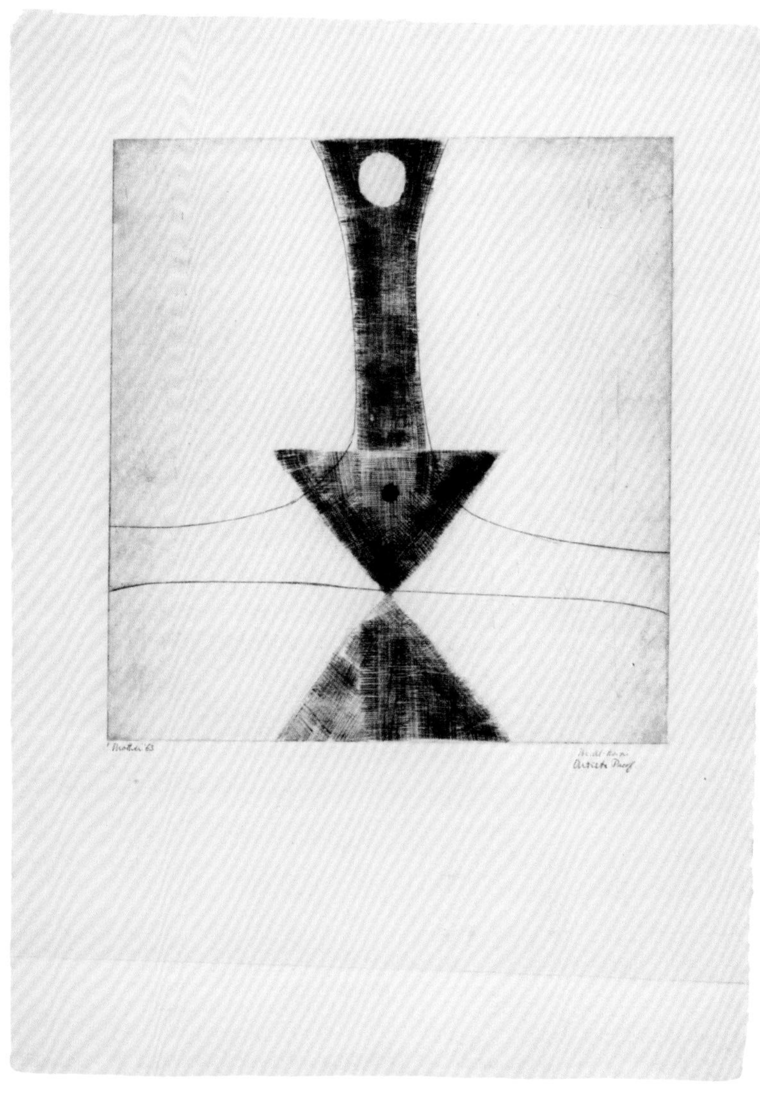

Lancelot Ribeiro 1933–2010
Cityscape (Night) 1963

Cityscape (Night) depicts a starlit sky above an urban landscape. Lancelot Ribeiro recurrently painted landscapes; this work arguably conveys a set of feelings related to the city of London, where Ribeiro had resettled in 1962 after an extended period spent in his birthplace, Bombay. With its expansive sky, twinkling stars and buildings teeming with life and excitement, *Cityscape (Night)* evokes the sense of optimism with which Ribeiro and his fellow international modernists arrived (or, in this case, arrived again) in London, a sentiment linked to their status as, in cultural theorist Stuart Hall's words, 'the last "colonials"': those who 'knew "Britain" intimately but from afar' and who 'came to see for themselves, to look it in the eye – and, if possible, to conquer it'.[11] Tellingly, in this respect, the artist signs his name among the stars. At the same time, the artwork can be read for the darkness that characterised life in London for Ribeiro and his peers, as described in the introduction to this book. Ribeiro later recalled 'days and nights spent in anguish and tears' during his early years in the city, which he had 'never forgotten'.[12] Capturing this, perhaps, in the overwhelming sense of the unknown in *Cityscape (Night)*'s sky, and the precarity of the urban environment, these responses among Ribeiro and his wider artistic network connected with a broader migrant sentiment discussed in relation to Avinash Chandra's painting *Hills of Gold* 1964 (see p.35). By giving form to the ambivalence – optimism matched by fear – felt during this historical turning point, *Cityscape (Night)* might be pinpointed as Ribeiro's contribution to what writer Sukhdev Sandhu has called a 'black metrography' of London, whereby 'immigrants . . . give shape and meaning to a metropolis that at first terrifies them'.[13]

Oil paint on board

122 x 91.6

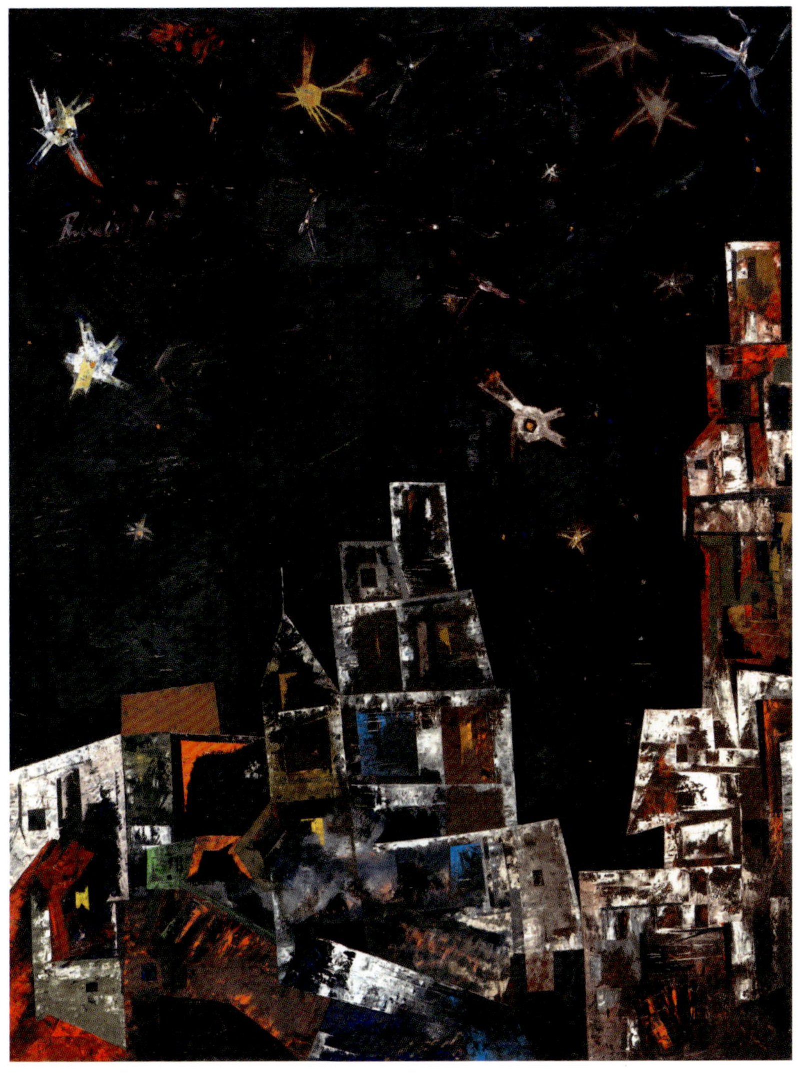

Avinash Chandra 1931–91
Hills of Gold 1964

Avinash Chandra believed in a conception of the artist as a
bearer of social responsibility, once stating that his concern
was not figuration for its own sake, but using figuration as
a vehicle for expressing 'all those things which are part of
you, which are around you or which you have left behind'.[14]
The layers of ambiguity in *Hills of Gold* suggest that this
commitment to social reality was matched by an aspiration
to universal resonance. The work is a long, horizontal painting
depicting an abundance of indeterminate forms
(is it a landscape comprising a bright red substratum, a layer
of hills and a dramatic climate on top, or is it an enormous
reclining nude 'caressed by an invisible lover'?).[15] The title at
once evokes Chandra's birthplace, the hill station of Simla,
but it also calls to mind Britain's status in the imagination of
postcolonial migrants (alluding both to 'streets paved with
gold' and the 'clouded hills' of 'Jerusalem'). If this is then an
indeterminate place encompassing both Britain and the homeland, it is
one fraught with ambivalence: rich and golden with promise, full of whirling
trajectories, yet offset by an unsettling force in the top-right corner of the
painting: a 'sun' rendered in icy blue, emitting a harsh, cold heat. This might
have reflected the contemporary, conflictual sentiments of expatriated
Indian artists in Britain, but it also resonated with a broader, generational
feeling of unease among postcolonial migrants in Britain at the turn of the
1960s, in the wake of the enforcement of increasingly racialised immigration
policy, anti-immigrant riots and a surge in racist attacks.

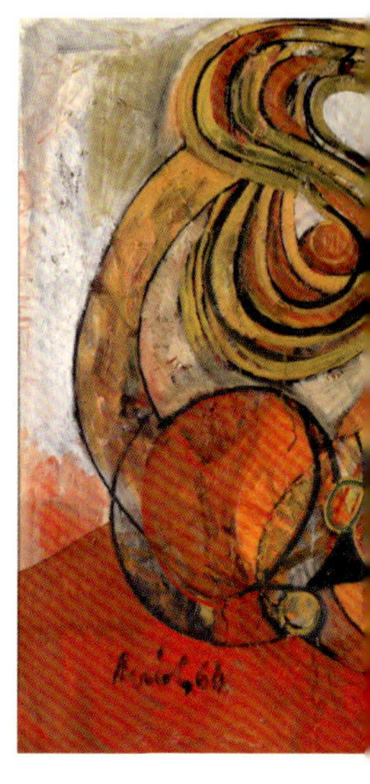

Oil paint on canvas
101.6 x 241.3

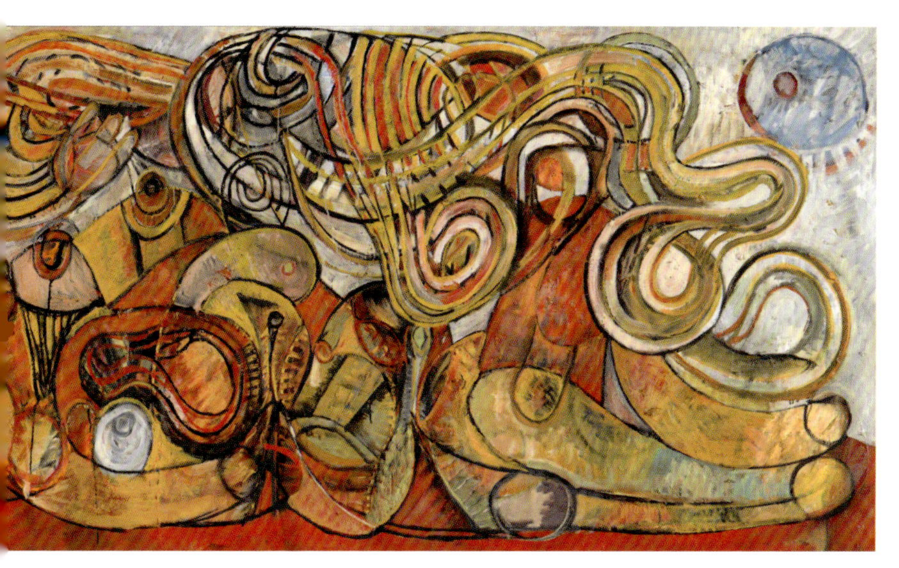

Ahmed Parvez 1926–79
Waiting for the Cloud 1964

Ahmed Parvez painted *Waiting for the Cloud* in 1964, the year that he ended
his period in London, where he had been living since leaving Lahore in 1955.
It is a small gouache painting, loosely resembling a landscape: a delicate
application of grey paint in the lower half evokes an urban environment,
while the upper half consists of a blue sky suffused with a warm, yellow
light. The dominant form in the painting is a bold brushstroke that surges
upwards before exploding into a constellation of splatters, shards and
expressive marks. *Waiting for the Cloud* resonates strongly with the artist's
1965 description of his experience of being in his studio in London: 'In a
cloudy place like London where . . . the world seems dull and downcast,
by chance the sun may come out. In a situation like that people may rush
into the parks, but I . . . open my studio window and shout, "There . . . is the
incredible miracle of the sun."' Parvez goes on to describe how this climatic
shift would provide a catalyst for an energetic painting session.[16] In *Waiting
for the Cloud*, the flood of sunshine and firework-like form, which soars
above the 'dullness', visualise such a moment; yet, the work's title, and the
looming form of a spectral cloud in the upper part of the composition,
foreshadow the return of melancholic weather. This inherent tension in the
work might be read – in conjunction with the works of Avinash Chandra
(p.35) and Lancelot Ribeiro (p.33) in this book – as ramifying to reflect a
shared sense among ex-colonial expatriated artists in London that the city
provoked both inspiration and dejection, and indeed a widespread feeling of
unease among racial minorities in the early 1960s.

Gouache on paper
33 x 17.8

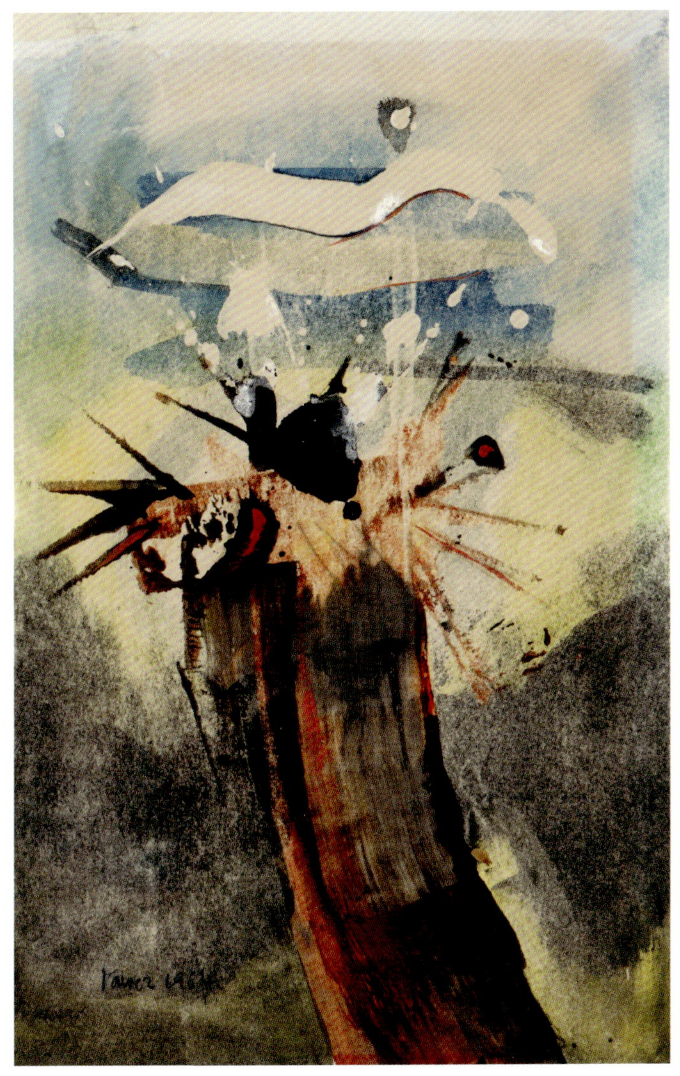

Anwar Jalal Shemza 1928–85
Meem Two 1967

Anwar Jalal Shemza uprooted himself from Lahore to study at the Slade School of Fine Art, London, in 1956. There, he attended a lecture by art historian Ernst Gombrich on the putatively 'functional' nature of Islamic art, which would become one impetus for the artist's lifelong pursuit of reconciling an Islamic frame of reference with an international modernist idiom of geometric abstraction – and drawing out the latter's historical inspiration from the former. To this end, *Meem Two* represents the Arabic letter meem four times: twice with the stem departing from the top of the canvas, and twice from the bottom. Shemza straightens out the sinuous lines of Islamic calligraphy to create rigid forms, and the four letters also create a set of positive and negative geometric shapes. Viewed alongside other works in Shemza's *Meem* series – in which the letters assume a vegetal quality – *Meem Two* is notable for its proximity to industrial visual and sensorial experience: the grey tones evoke concrete and steel, as well as smog.[17] Meanwhile, the ziggurat shape of the central form recalls the Empire State Building: a metonym for capitalist progress, and a symbol of the city on which Shemza's generation had its sights as the new centre of cultural modernity during this period (both Avinash Chandra and F.N. Souza moved there from London in 1967). Therefore, *Meem Two* arguably raised questions of the colonial politics of art historical discourse, and of trans-cultural modernism, in relation to the industrial dimension of modernity. Remarkably, Shemza's deep and sustained reflection on transversal modernity took place from the relative detachment of his home in Stafford, where he had settled in 1961.

Oil paint on canvas
91.5 x 91.5

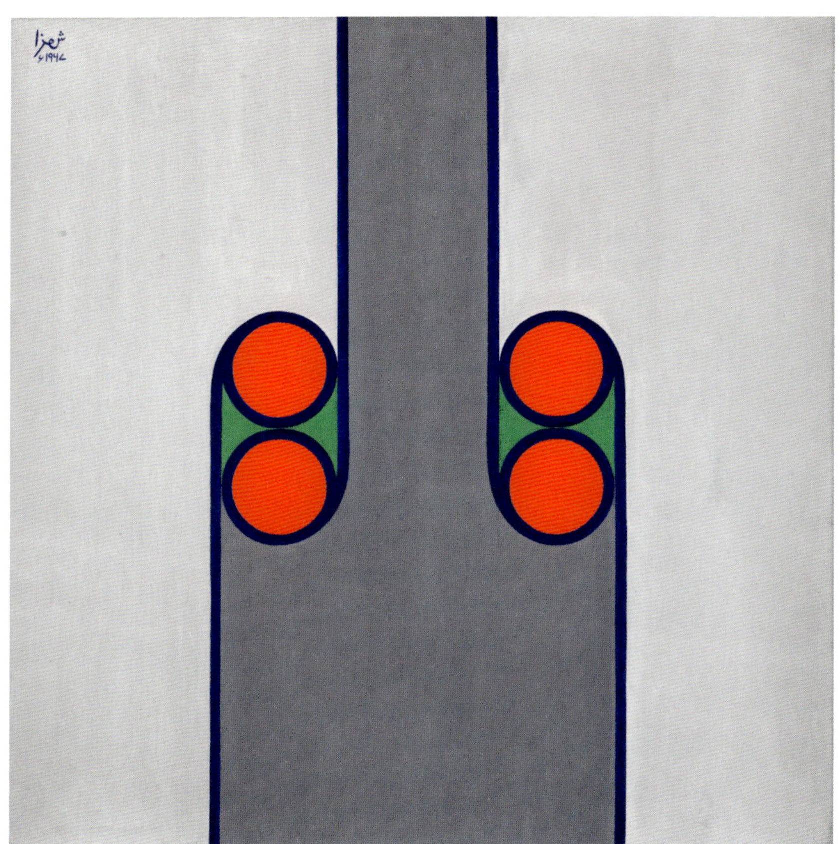

Maria Souza 1914–95
Possibly a sketch for a silk velvet dress with Rajasthani mirror embellishment c.1970s

Maria Souza relocated to London from Bombay (now Mumbai) in 1950, following her husband, F.N. Souza. There she established a bespoke dressmaking service, producing clothes that were on-trend, yet elaborated to make bolder statements, while also exhibiting technical prowess. An example is a dress made by Souza for actress Joanna Lumley, which adopts the then fashionable tiered bubble dress design, while adding extra tiers to increase impact and showcase the maker's ability to handle challenging construction. According to fashion historian Bethan Bide, Souza contributed to the revolutionisation of high fashion in postwar London, which saw a range of designers claim the title of bespoke dressmaker, mounting a challenge to the gatekeeping of court dressmakers. At the same time, Souza's emphasis on execution showed a certain loyalty to the old order.[18] Souza worked on a reference-only basis, for clients including then editor-in-chief of *British Vogue*, Ailsa Garland, and film stars such as Lumley. For Bide, Souza's use of networking to develop her clientele demonstrated a powerful ability to 'articulate the transformational promise of fashion'.[19] As mentioned in the introduction, from 1975 to 1985, Souza also ran the art gallery Arts 38 from her residence at 38 Homer Street in London's West End. There she operated 'an international gallery for unestablished artists', including promotion of the work of her (by now) ex-husband.[20] Souza's practice as a gallerist also included co-running the Horizon Gallery, active on Marchmont Street in Bloomsbury from 1987 to 1991. Despite Souza's importance as a dressmaker, networker and gallerist in twentieth-century London, this text is one of only a handful of accounts of her work that have been published to date.

Pencil on paper

29.7 x 21

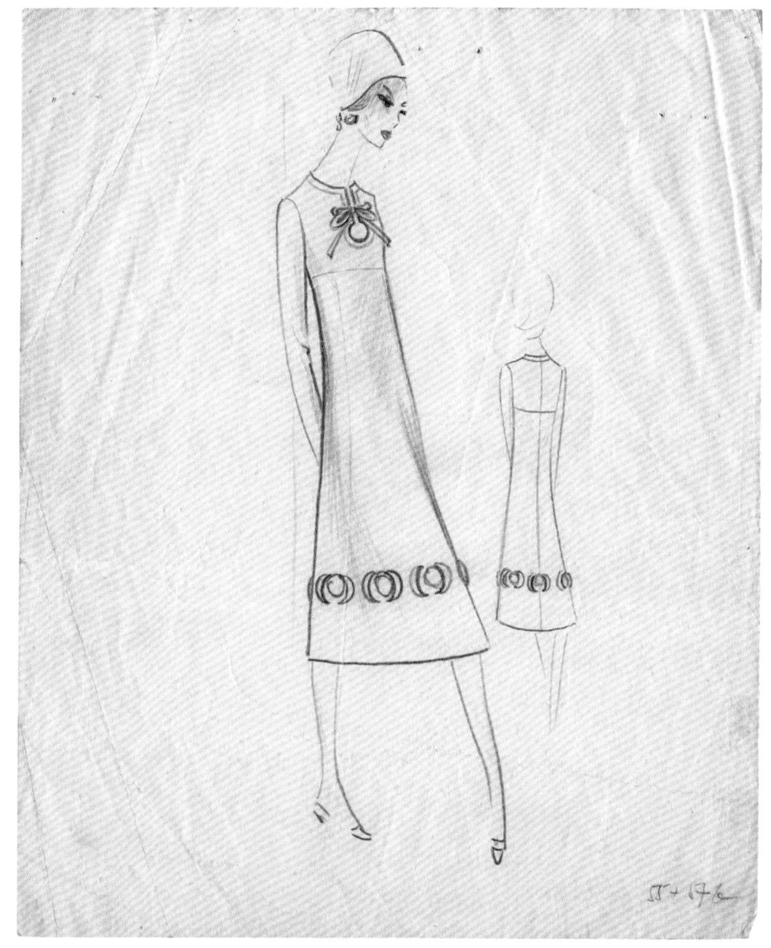

Rasheed Araeen b.1935
Fire! 1975, printed 1984

Rasheed Araeen's *Fire!* formed part of the endeavour, articulated in his
watershed 1978 text 'Preliminary Notes for a BLACK MANIFESTO', to
develop 'an art which embraces the radical consciousness of its time' –
specifically, an anti-colonial and anti-racist aesthetic.[21] *Fire!* focuses on
the victory of the People's Army of Vietnam in 1975 – indeed, it was first
exhibited at a festival by the collective Artists for Democracy, which aimed
to celebrate the defeat of the US and South Vietnamese government forces.
The artwork comprises a grid of twenty-four black-and-white photographs
arranged in a sequence proceeding from left to right. The first image is of a
sheet of blank paper; then, a drawing of a US flag emerges, but with fifty-two
warplanes and the letter 'B' replacing the stars (code for the B-52 bomber
used by US forces in Vietnam). Then, 'AMERICAN IMPERIALISM' is written in
pseudo-official typeface on the flag, followed by the addition of insurgent
graffiti reading 'DOWN WITH'. The artist's hand introduces a portrait of
the president Ho Chi Minh into the frame, and a lit match is brought to the
page, burning through the flag to reveal a photograph of Liberation Front
fighters inset into a flag of the National Liberation Front of South Vietnam.
Finally, the artist's hand enters a star into the frame; from a retrospective
vantage point, this may connote, in the words of art historian Kylie Gilchrist,
the survival of 'structures of enmity and nationalist aggression' in south-
east Asia after the defeat of US forces.[22] Araeen's deployment of fire as a
medium to represent redevelopments in what we might describe as the
war of position against imperialism and nationalisms is one of many cases in
which his oeuvre uses burning as an illustration and perhaps enactment of
social transformation.

---

24 photographs, C-prints on paper, mounted on foam
Each 30 x 45.3

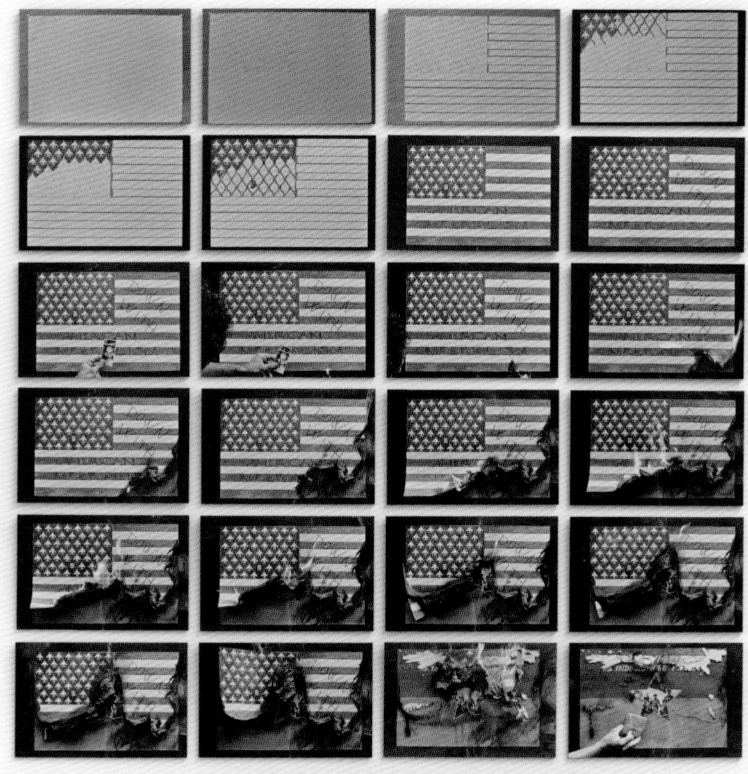

Mount Pleasant Photography Workshop
Untitled c.1980s

The Southampton-based Mount Pleasant Photography Workshop (MPPW) was
made up of photographers aged between eight and twelve, brought together
and supported by photographer and educator Judy Harrison.[23] It emerged from
Harrison's background in socialist photography cultures, and from contemporary
multiculturalist activism in education. It began with Harrison's fellowship at
Southampton Photographic Gallery in 1977. Given an open brief to work with
photography and children, she based herself at Mount Pleasant Middle School,
where the majority of pupils were Black and South Asian. She then grew the project
until MPPW was established as an independent, community-run entity in 1982.
Photographers at MPPW learned the entire process of making photographs, and
enjoyed ownership over the equipment and facilities necessary to undertake it,
as well as staging exhibitions and making educational resources. This photograph
by Sucha Singh Digwa (b.1970) is set in a living room. With a palpable feeling of
love and kinship towards the sitters, Digwa depicts a baby balancing on its father's
outstretched palm. The mother is in the background, having seemingly hurried
into place before the stunt was over. In line with the photographer's claim in their
magazine, *Step Forward*, that 'the use of photography has a very important role to
contribute in the promotion of anti-racism', Digwa's photograph tackles multiple
misconceptions about British South Asian communities.[24] To cite just one example, it
offers a dignified and humanising portrait of a man wearing a turban, where turbans
were historically seen as inhibitors to South Asian integration. Yet, the disruptions
of racialising cultural representations carried out by photographs were only part of
MPPW's socio-cultural significance. Equally important was that the photographs were
produced through what photography theorist Christopher Pinney calls a 'developing
craft-community': a formation committed to localism and openness.[25]

35mm film
40.6 x 50.8

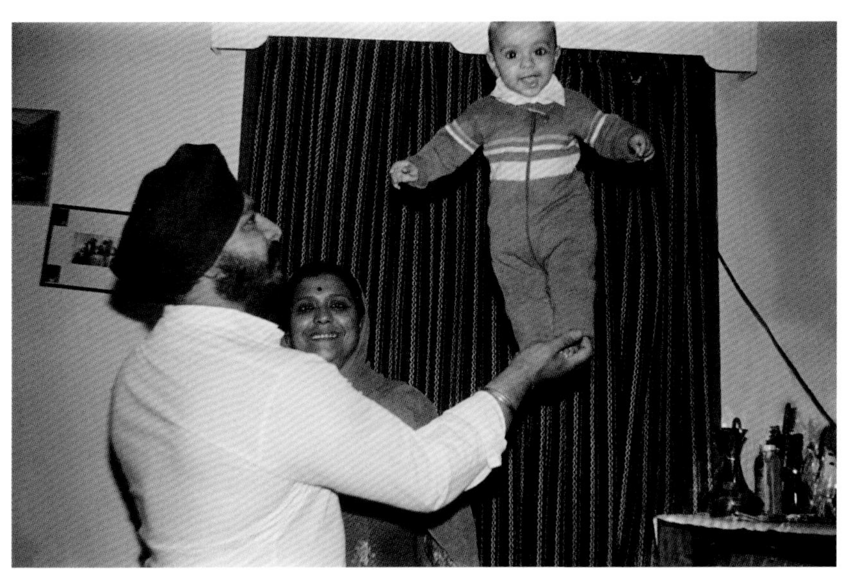

Jamil Dehlavi b.1944
The Blood of Hussain 1980

The epigraph of *The Blood of Hussain*, 'to the people of Pakistan',
might be taken as that of Jamil Dehlavi's broader oeuvre – though the
filmmaker has substantially lived in political exile. *The Blood of Hussain*
represents a rebellion against a military regime in Pakistan led by Hussain,
the son of a landowner, who gives up his privileges to live alongside his
compatriots. The film draws an allegorical connection to the Battle of
Karbala (680 CE), in which the Prophet Muhammad's grandson Hussain
rose up against the tyrannical Yazid, as memorialised by Shi'i Muslims in
a rich dramaturgical tradition each year.[26] *The Blood of Hussain* opens
with scenes of the commemoration of Karbala in Lahore and ends by
collapsing its contemporary and historical narratives, as Hussain charges
into battle despite being vastly outnumbered, and is martyred. In the first
instance, the film is a call to action against political repression in Pakistan
in its immediate moment: one month after filming concluded, the military
coup and establishment of martial law under Zia-al-Haq took place. Dehlavi
soon fled to London, where he released *The Blood of Hussain*, having made
edits to link it with its immediate political context – including the addition
of a speech by Zia. Moreover, as curator Ali Nobil Ahmad argues, like the
memory of Karbala, the film's call to action might also relate beyond its
particular moment to other struggles of resistance against oppression.[27]
Indeed, the film closes with Hussain's white stallion (evocative of Zuljanah,
the steed of the Prophet's grandson), now lone on the battlefield, galloping
towards the viewer, in search of a new rider to continue the struggle.
However, a contradiction within the film is the lack of power exercised by
female characters, and its uneven distribution along racial lines.

35mm film
112 min

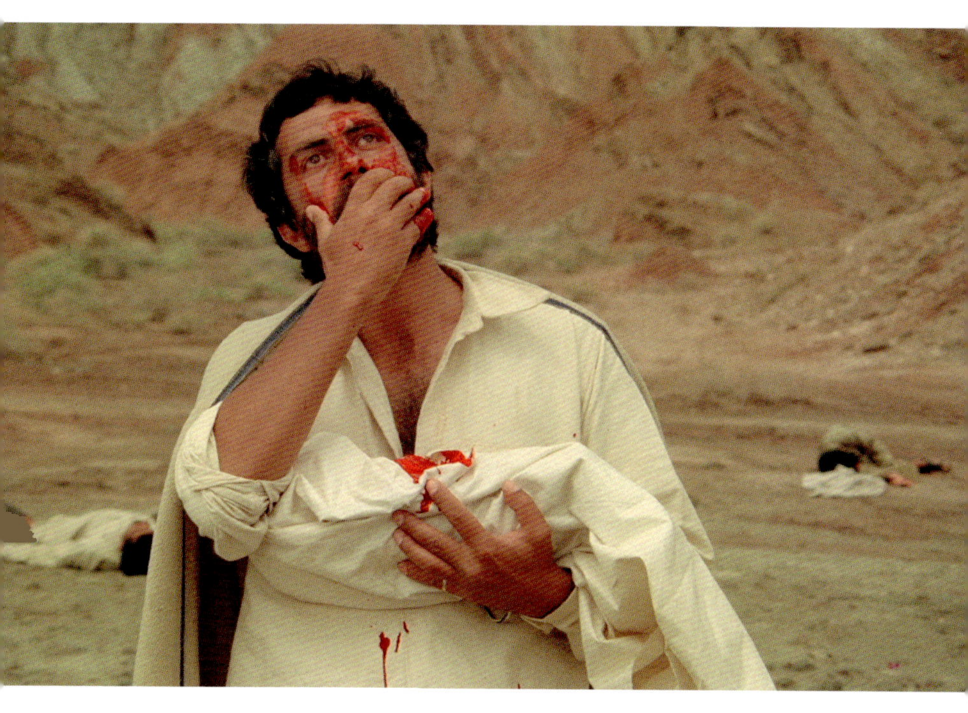

Shafique Uddin b.1962
Relatives Gather at the Dead Woman's House;
She Became Ill and Died Suddenly 1980

Relatives Gather at the Dead Woman's House; She Became Ill and Died Suddenly represents a woman's passage from the mortal world to the afterlife, according to Islamic doctrine. The deceased is at the centre of the composition. Her wide-open eye indicates that her transit is an active process. A luminescent, blue cloud around her head represents the afterlife beckoning her, while a supine figure on her front might be Azra'il, the angel of death, drawing out her soul. Surrounding the deceased, as the title indicates, are her relatives, variously holding a talisman over her body, reaching towards her or gesticulating. Shafique Uddin's use of riotous colour, and abbreviated brushstrokes, convey the drama and energy of this pivotal, divine moment, which sweeps up, and diffuses itself across, the entire surrounding landscape and figures. Like many of Uddin's paintings, this might be read as the expression of a memory from his childhood in Sylhet, Bangladesh, before he migrated to London in the 1970s. Yet the depiction of the passage between life and the afterlife might also be taken as an analogy for the transitory spatio-temporal state of migrancy. As historian Ranajit Guha describes, since 'it is in their everyday dealings with one another that people in any society form such links in a present which continually assimilates the past to itself as experience and looks forward at the same time to a future secure for all', the migrant's 'loss of that present amounts, therefore, to a loss of the world in which the migrant has had his [*sic*] own identity forged. Ousted temporally no less than spatially, he [*sic*] will, henceforth, be adrift until he [*sic*] lands in a second world where his [*sic*] place will seek and hopefully find matching coordinates again in a time he[*sic*], like others, should be able to claim as *"our* time".'[28]

Tempera, coloured crayons and mixed media on paper
47 x 60.5

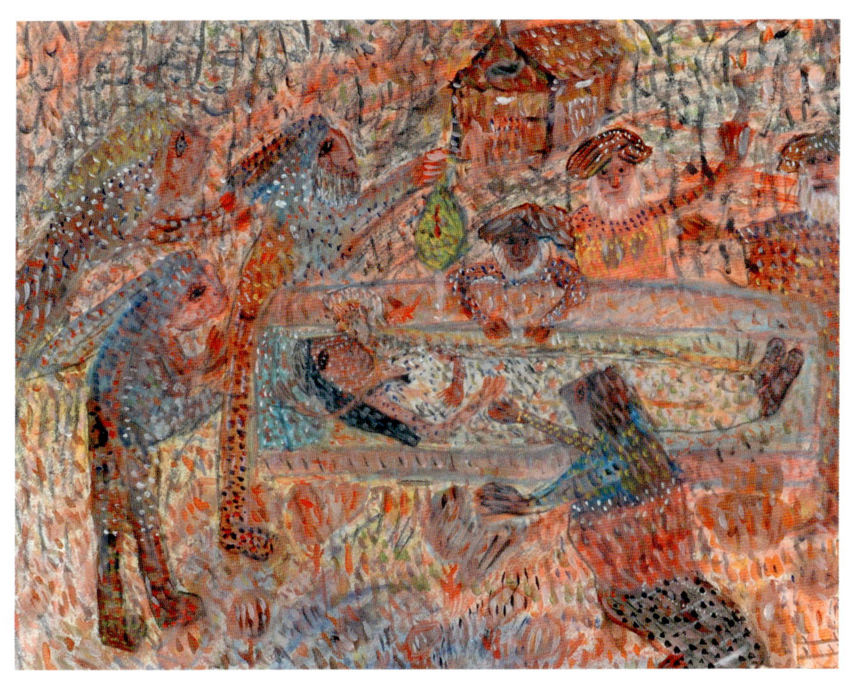

Yugesh Walia b.1954
Mirror, Mirror 1980

Yugesh Walia's short film *Mirror, Mirror* depicts a South Asian woman, named Jo, attempting to carve out a space for herself and to seek refuge from the racial and patriarchal pressures she faces from British society and the South Asian community. We see Jo spending an evening alone in her friend's apartment, receiving equally hostile calls from her family and white boyfriend, which reverberate in her internal monologue. We then see her wake up in a cold sweat from a dream in which she is the ideal picture of South Asian femininity, before the film ends with her despairing, her head buried in her hands. Though it does not deliver a happy ending, the film is not without hope: over the course of the evening, we also see Jo make dhal for dinner, enjoy the untranslatable romance of the title song from *Kabhi Kabhie*, and listen to Fleetwood Mac (additionally a wink from Walia gesturing to South Asian cultures of 'rumour') – an indication of the possibility of her making a space that will accommodate the multitudes and contradictions of her diasporic subjectivity. In Walia's view, *Mirror, Mirror* was an outsider's perspective on South Asian femininity in 1980s Britain, made shortly after his arrival in Birmingham from Delhi to study at the Birmingham School of Photography in 1976, when he unexpectedly found himself in a concentrated site of both racism and anti-racist struggle. It also bears the mark of his engagement with a longstanding socialist and anti-racist film and photography culture in Birmingham. This included his photography course, which placed importance on 'knowing what a media does and understanding the world it lives in', and local collectives such as Birmingham Film and Video Workshop, which enabled marginalised people 'to create a space in which they were foregrounded'.[29]

Production still
16mm film 23 min

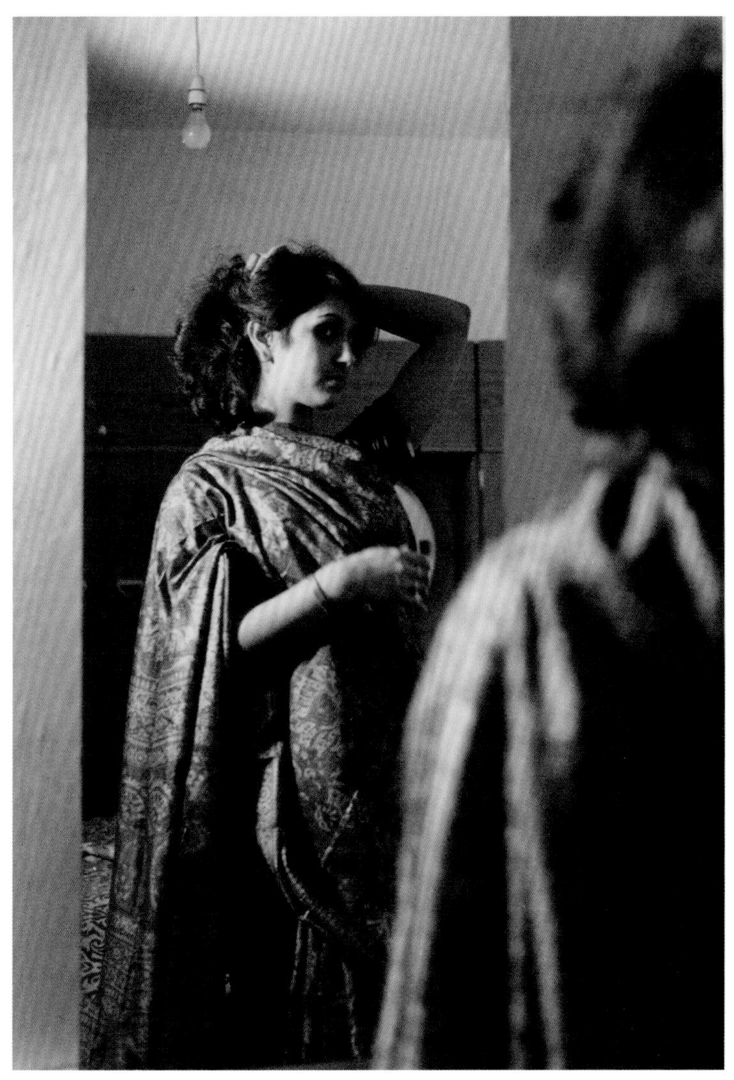

Chila Kumari Singh Burman b.1957
Cut – Foot – Pupil – Uprisings 1981–2

Part of the *Riot* series of prints, *Cut – Foot – Pupil – Uprisings* is inextricable
from the political moment of its making: the anti-racist uprisings of the turn
of the 1980s.[30] *Cut – Foot – Pupil – Uprisings* is a before-and-after diptych,
representing state violence on the one hand, and the resistance it triggered
on the other. The left-hand print comprises a photo of a policeman overlaid
with a red dressmaking pattern, strategically arranged so that a double-
ended arrow symbolically decapitates the officer. This print is titled 'SHOTS',
the double meaning of which (gunshots and photographs) points to the
two, complicit violences of direct contact with state forces and of racism
in the media (a key site of intervention for Chila Burman and the emergent
British Black Arts Movement, in which she was involved). The right-hand
print, meanwhile, is titled 'Uprising'. It is identical to its counterpart, except
that the image of the policeman appears corroded – produced by the artist
soaking the etching plate in acid: a violent effect of a violent process.[31] This
corrosion both reproduces the political rage expressed during the uprisings,
and shows off the uprisings' political wins: eroding the claims of the police
force to respectability or good faith.[32] Yet *Cut – Foot – Pupil – Uprisings*
sustains momentum: its inclusion of media of reproduction and mass action
(the photograph, the print, the sewing pattern – even the title looks like a
'cut along the dotted line' pictogram) spur the viewer to join the ongoing
struggle for liberation.

Photo-etching and screenprint on paper
Each 72 x 49.8

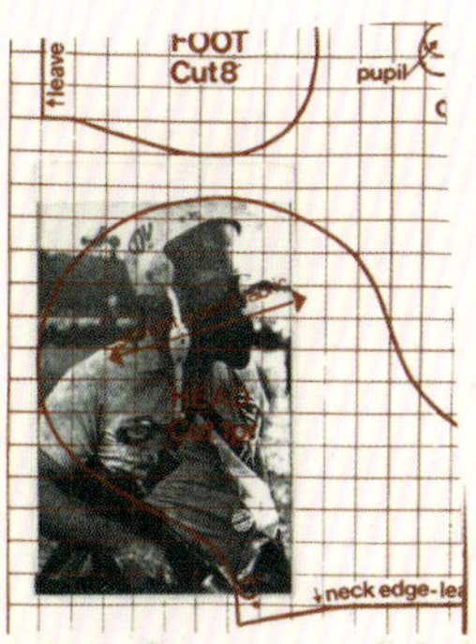
FOOT
Cut 8
leave
pupil
HEAD
neck edge-lea

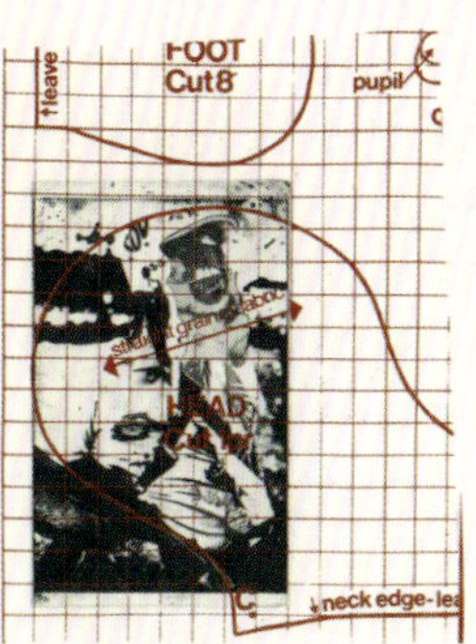
FOOT
Cut 8
leave
pupil
shallow grain labour
HEAD
neck edge-lea

Black Audio Film Collective
Expeditions 1: Signs of Empire 1982–4

The Black Audio Film Collective (John Akomfrah, Lina Gopaul, Reece
Auguiste, Avril Johnson, Trevor Mathison, Edward George, David Lawson
and Claire Joseph) was a group that produced experimental films and
a programme of cine-cultural activity from 1982 to 1998. The members
were of diverse heritages, including African, African Caribbean and Indian
Caribbean, and the 'Black' in their name adopted the contemporary
organisation of transcultural anti-racist coalitions using 'black' political
identity.[33] *Expeditions 1: Signs of Empire* is part of an early, two-part
slide-tape project. It stages an encounter between Britain's imperial past,
and then present anxieties about the children of empire in the former
metropole (such as the collective members). It consists of a tape loop
of slides, each comprising a fragment from the imperial archive, such as
jingoistic children's books or photographs of hunting trophies. These
images are overlaid with a poem – rendered in Letraset – that at some
points fabulates colonised subjects speaking back to their oppressors:
'"Where is God?" said the black girl | to the missionary who had converted
her'. Meanwhile, the film's soundtrack loops a hollow speech praising British
imperial unity, and a then recent comment by QC Sir Ronald Bell, aired
on BBC's *Panorama*, that the anti-racist uprisings of the turn of the 1980s
demonstrated that young diasporic Britons 'don't know who they are or
what they are'. Auguiste later wrote that this dismembering and reassembly
of Britain's imperial history and racially charged present was a hopeful set
of gestures: 'every new piece of film that we retrieved from the archives
presented us with new possibilities of deconstruction and simultaneously
the reconstruction of both past and present.'[34]

Photographic test
Single–channel 35mm colour Ektachrome transferred to video and sound 26 min

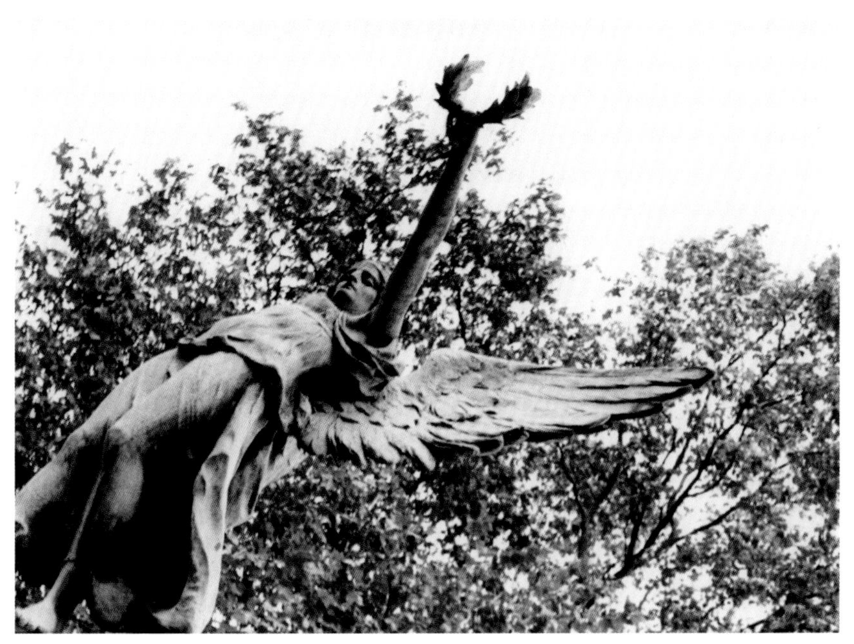

Symrath Patti b.1961
Black Skin White Masks 1983

Black Skin White Masks is a black-and-white photographic portrait of Symrath
Patti, taken by her then partner, and fellow fine art student, Raj Batra. Patti is
draped in a black cloth, and bedecked in South Asian jewellery. On her hand, in
mehndi, she bears reproductions of the hammer and sickle and of a swastika: a
Hindu sign appropriated by National Socialism as a symbol of Aryan supremacy,
and, in the period in which *Black Skin White Masks* was produced, taken up
as a wider racist symbol. A stripe of white paint vertically bisects Patti's face,
suggesting the 'white mask' of her title, which cites psychiatrist and anti-colonial
activist Frantz Fanon's book *Black Skin, White Masks* 1952, exploring the effects
of racialisation on psychic and embodied existence. At the time, Patti was
emerging into activist cultures that espoused the adoption of oppositional
political identities, drawing from influences such as *Black Power: The Politics
of Liberation in America* 1967, in which Kwame Ture and Charles V. Hamilton
argued that forging an 'energetic, determined, intelligent, beautiful and peace-
loving' black political identity would produce 'group solidarity and identity for
the purpose of attaining certain goals in the body politic'.[35] Reflecting the artist's
contemporaneous political development, *Black Skin White Masks* can be read
as staging the process of politicisation, and of advocating identity formation as
a political act in itself. The artist's act of wrapping herself in black cloth might
be read as a signifier for the contemporary transcultural adoption of 'black'
political identity. The wound cloth rhymes with the partially rolled canvas in
the background, which states an artistic commitment to the broader struggle.
By wearing mehndi and jewellery, she makes space for the culture of 'home' in
public. Finally, the work's title, and its visualisation in the artist's make-up, affirms
the importance of radical literature in oppositional identity formation.

35mm film
61 x 50.8

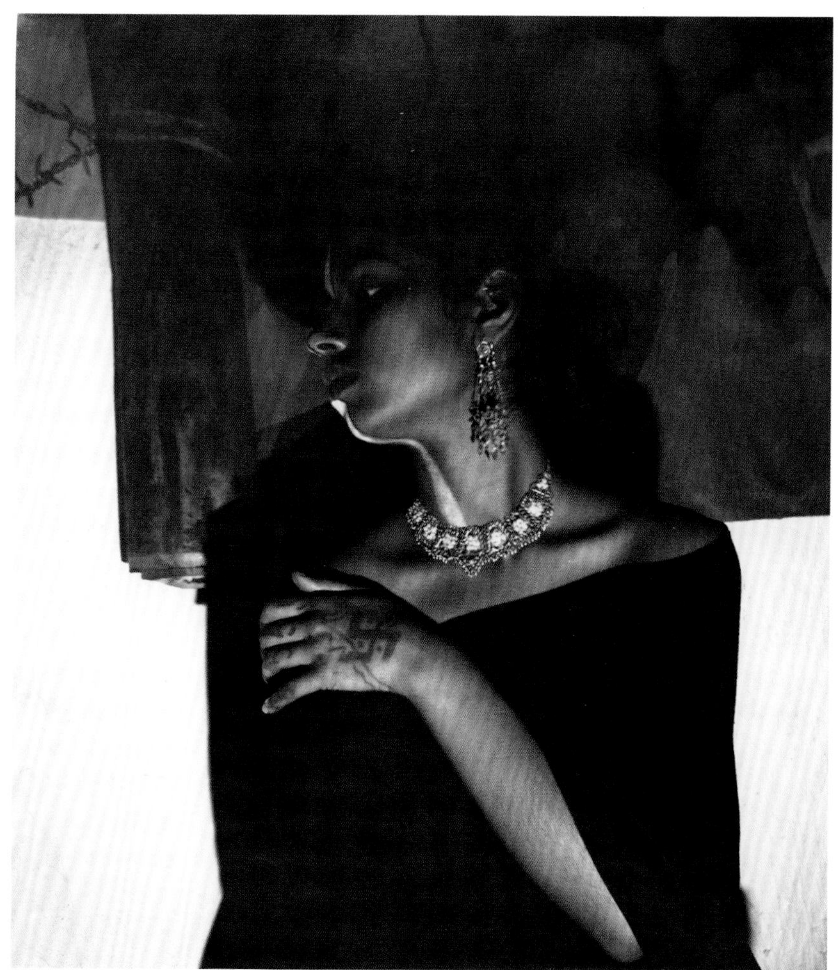

Sutapa Biswas b.1962
Housewives with Steak-Knives 1983–5

Housewives with Steak-Knives is a colossal depiction of Kali, goddess of
destruction and renewal. Here, she wields a machete; a severed head; a flower;
and a flag consisting of photocopies of Artemisia Gentileschi's paintings
of Judith slaying Holofernes – illustrations in Griselda Pollock's and Rozsika
Parker's landmark work of feminist art history, *Old Mistresses: Women, Art
and Ideology* 1981.[36] *Housewives with Steak-Knives* critiqued a tendency in the
Women's Liberation Movement to uphold the white woman as its universal
subject. Arguably, Sutapa Biswas confronted this whiteness by offering the
movement Kali, a figure for coalitional thought and practice developed in the
context of British South Asian feminist activism. South Asian feminists made
prolific representations of Kali as a way of claiming their own visual signifier,
and therefore symbolically carving out an autonomous organising space.
Depicting Kali enabled the forging of figurative links with anti-racist activists
of South Asian heritage who expressed their commitment to a transcultural
coalition organised by 'black' political identity by using the term 'kala' ('black'
in several South Asian languages) in their protest cultures, since 'kali' is the
feminine form of 'kala'.[37] Further, portraying Kali enabled British South Asian
feminists to symbolically connect themselves to the Women's Liberation
Movement, which, particularly within feminist spirituality circles, embraced Kali
as a matriarchal deity. In *Housewives with Steak-Knives*, Biswas brought Kali
to contemporary feminists as a figure representing the necessary yet difficult
work of coalitional negotiation on axes of race and gender. This could be put
towards building 'unity among women and across geographical spaces and
cultures', which the artist argued was necessary to overthrow the tyrannical
regimes of men.[38]

Acrylic paint, pastel and photocopy collage on paper, mounted on canvas
274 x 244

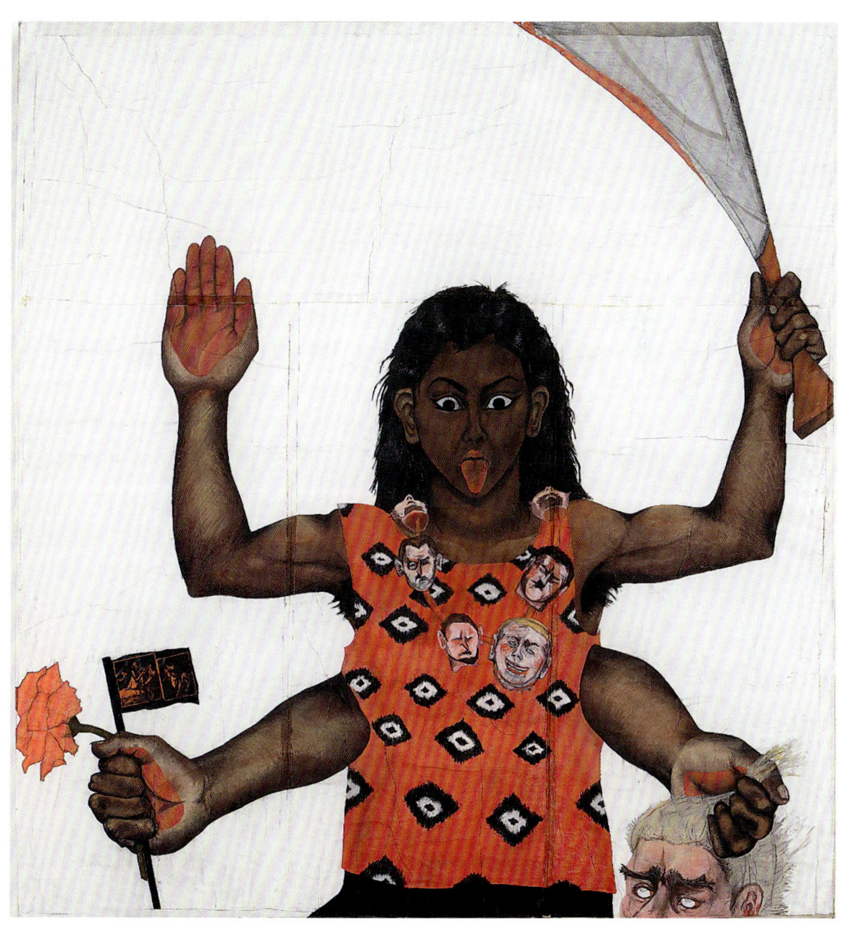

Prodeepta Das b.1948
Bonda Women, Malkangiri, Odisha from the series *The Hill of Flutes: Images of Odisha* 1984

Prodeepta Das's practice is driven by what he calls 'an interest in people'.[39] This core motivation first impelled the artist to enrol in an undergraduate degree in social anthropology (for which he moved from his birthplace, Orissa (now Odisha), to Sussex in 1968), before taking up documentary photography. Historically, both anthropology and photography were marked by asymmetries in power between the observer and the object of study – relations which were being supplanted by critical methodologies in the era in which Das began practising. Notably, his engagement with the critical traditions of socialist and anti-racist photography in Britain led him to organise an exhibition of contemporary British South Asian photographers, titled *Darshan*, at Camerawork in London in 1986. *The Hill of Flutes*, which was exhibited at the same venue in 1987, exemplifies Das's humanistic, critical documentary ethos. The occasion for the series was Das's invitation by social anthropologist Sitakant Mahapatra to accompany him on a visit to five Adivasi communities in Orissa, where Mahapatra would translate the communities' oral poems, and Das would take photographs for publication alongside them. In this work, Das offers an empowering depiction of three people from the Bonda community: the camera is positioned below them each, enabling them to assume monumental, towering positions. One of the figures defiantly returns the viewer's gaze, while the others, equally magnanimous, raise their chins and look into the distance. This empowering representational ethos may be read as a statement of solidarity with the community's contemporary struggles against the transformation of its socio-economic organisation as a result of state-sponsored development programmes.[40]

Fujichrome colour transparency film
40.6 x 30.4

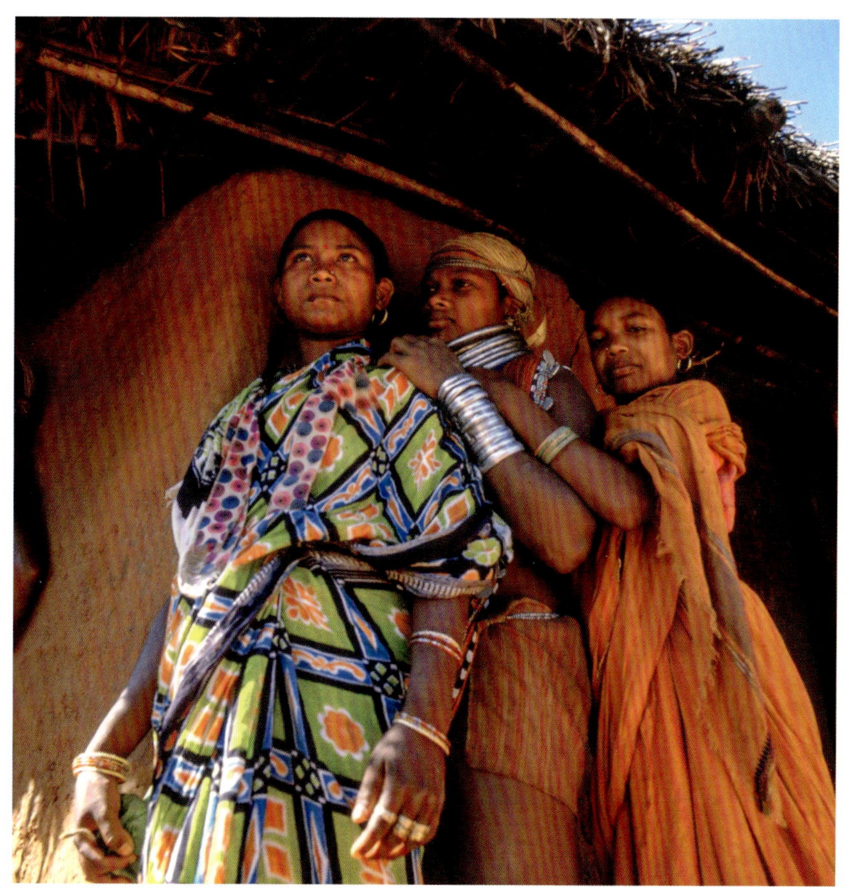

Retake Film and Video Collective
Majdhar 1984

Retake Film and Video Collective was co-founded in 1982 by brothers Ahmed and Mahmood Jamal. The first full-time workers of Retake were Sima Gill, Durriya Kazi and Sebastian Shah, before the later addition of Suman Bhuchar. Engaging with contemporary anti-racist movements and socially conscious filmmaking, Retake used film to challenge prejudiced cultural representations (hence the evocation of overwriting in the name), as well as undertaking crucial work to bring people of colour into the film and TV industries. Retake was franchised under the terms of the 1982 Workshop Declaration; this meant they received public funding and distribution on the newly launched Channel 4.[41] Retake's masterpiece was the feature film *Majdhar*. It tells the story of Fauzia, whose sole identity on arrival in London from Pakistan is that of a wife, as she goes through a process of self-actualisation. As film critic Swagato Chakravorty has argued, '*Majdhar* imagines a fully fleshed out world that was, for its time, radically at odds with popular imagery and representations of British Asian subjectivity. In *Majdhar*, we find images of South Asians living and working in England as fully realised, individual human beings.'[42] Indeed, much of the action takes place at the Pentonville Gallery in Bloomsbury, against the backdrop of a sleek café/bar and an exhibition of artworks by Rasheed Araeen (p.43). This setting signals British South Asians' location within the contemporary – not least as agents of cutting-edge political activism and culture. At the same time, *Majdhar* contested the internal politics of an externally homogenised 'Asian community'. Notably, Fauzia has an abortion, assuming ownership of her own body in the face of patriarchal demands, and there is a flirtation with inter-faith romance in her relationship with Arun.

Production still
16mm film 78 min

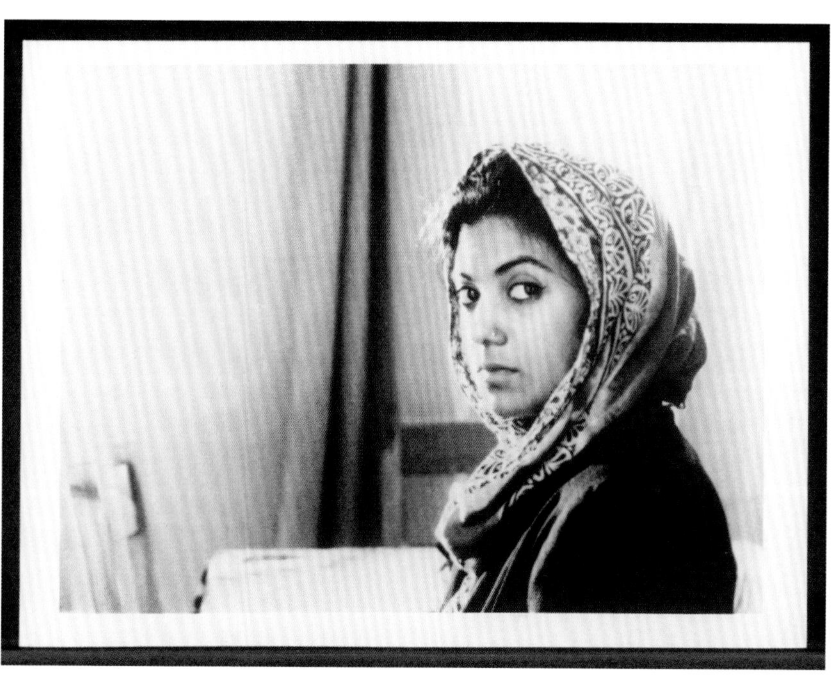

Nadir Tharani b.1952

Structure for the Commonwealth Institute's African Music Village, Holland Park, London 1984

This installation, commissioned by the Commonwealth Institute as part of its African Music Village in Holland Park, London, in 1984, consisted of a winding arrangement of upright timber posts, painted in the green, yellow and red of Pan-Africanism, as well as in the green, blue and yellow of the flag of Nadir Tharani's birthplace, Tanzania. The poles wove an unintrusive, yet visually intriguing and dynamic trajectory through the park, marking out the site of the music festival. In clusters that swell and contract, the installation has rhythm, befitting the sonic premise of the broader festival, which is enhanced by bands of yellow that cascade upwards and downwards across the poles. This photograph shows children interacting with the installation, swerving in and out of its gaps. This participatory element of the structure suggests a liberatory vision of aesthetic encounter aligned with Tharani's involvement in circles experimenting with reorienting cultural practice in the context of social struggles during the 1970s and 1980s. By inviting the viewer to activate this installation by mapping their own itineraries through it, Tharani's work mounts an implicit challenge to the social vision of the Commonwealth Institute itself. The latter advanced its conception of postcolonial social relations, as architectural historian Mark Crinson has argued, through the layout of its building. Ushered into a central space via a display providing information about Britain's relation to the Commonwealth, the visitor was 'interpellated as a British subject . . . who knows the Commonwealth only by being located within but not as part of its global ring, at a point where all its radii converge.'[43] Tharani's installation, by contrast, promoted an emancipatory and arguably democratic politics of space, characterised by openness, flexibility and improvisation.

Commercial timber posts and paint

4000 x 2000

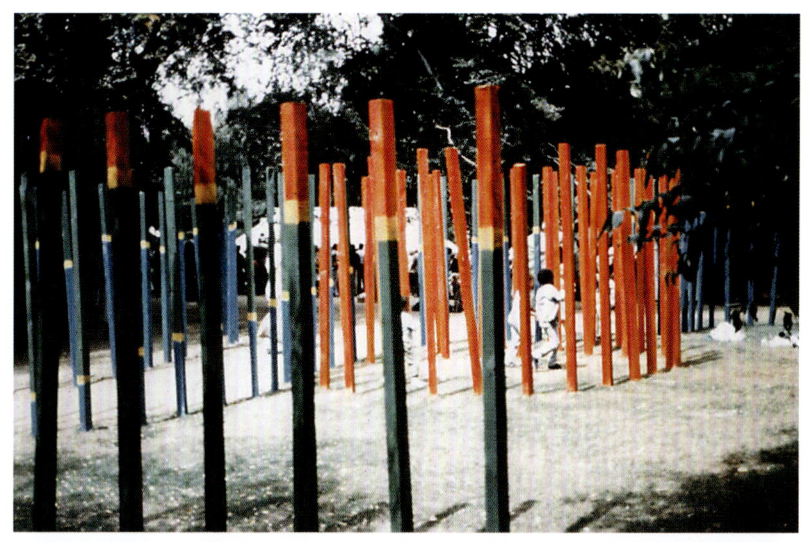

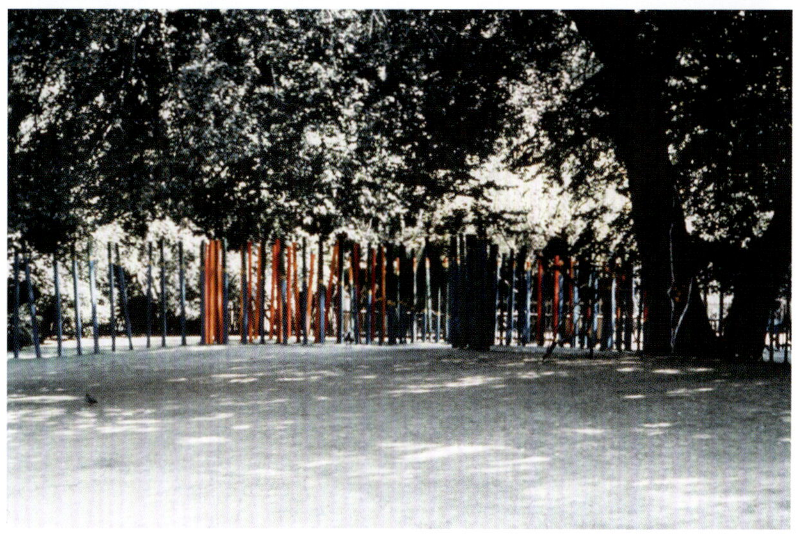

Shanti Thomas b.1949
The Voyagers 1984

The Voyagers exemplifies Shanti Thomas's description of the core tenets
of her artistic practice: 'My work begins from a perspective of you and
me . . . from there it ripples outward to encompass the family, society and
identity'; 'What interests me is . . . in effect, the human condition.'[44] Indeed,
the work allows us to read this as a rearticulation of the famous second-
wave feminist slogan 'the personal is political' (*The Voyagers* was made in
the same year that Thomas participated in the community-focused feminist
group exhibition *Fertile Eye*, organised by the Women's Work Collective, at
Brixton Art Gallery), one that is extended to broader, universal concerns.
The Voyagers depicts a man and a woman in a boat on roiling waters. The
man is stitching a net, while the woman's head is buried in a tangled pile
of ropes on a plank. Simultaneously, a bright light seems to be dawning
beyond the left edge of the canvas, causing the male figure to look up
from his activity, and the woman to raise her arm to shield her eyes. Here,
Thomas – who received her artistic training at the Academy of Fine Art
in Florence, and quotes Italian art history as key source material for her
work – might be citing the depiction of an eruption of light to symbolise
a moment of recognition in the work of Caravaggio. In Thomas's painting,
it possibly signifies a reckoning with men's entrapment of women under
patriarchy (symbolised by the net), and the prospect of escape or even
freedom, as symbolised by the plank and pile of ropes – though the latter
might also convey the woman's emotional turmoil. In the light of Thomas's
characterisation of her practice, the painting might also be read as ramifying
to proffer a meditation on ensnarement, escape and relationality at large.

Acrylic paint on paper
120.8 x 90

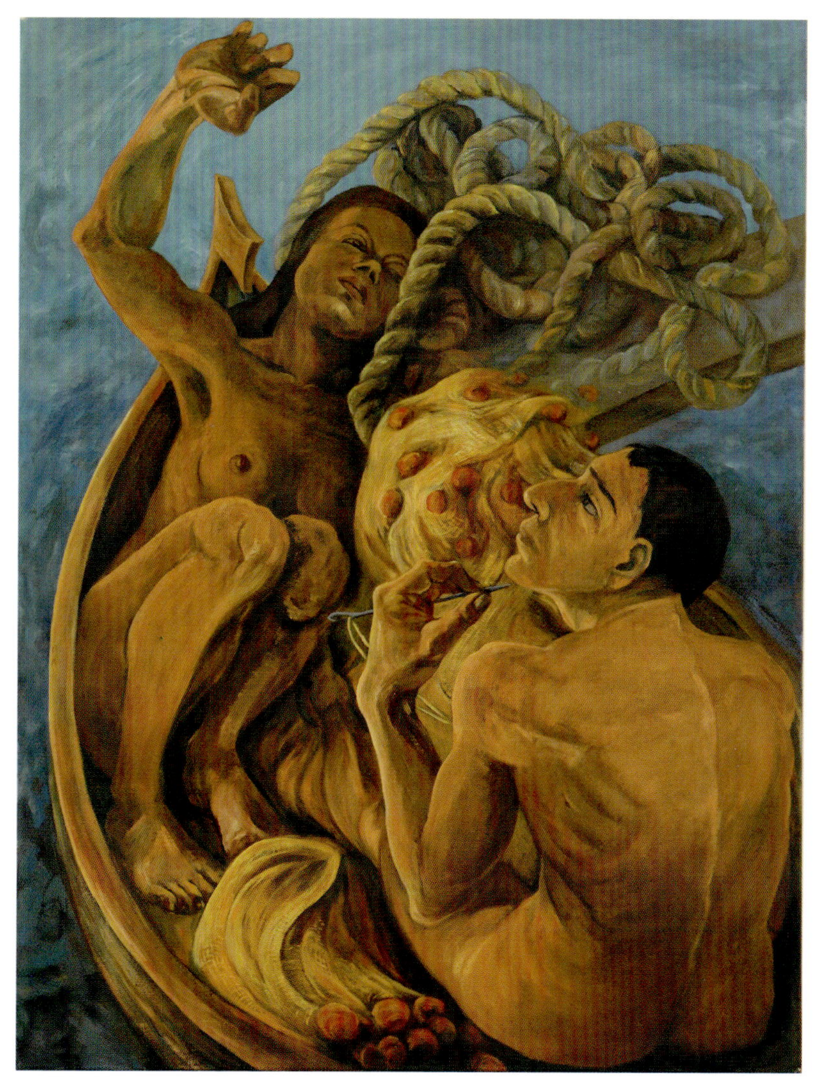

Ivan Peries 1921–88
Monk on the Seashore at Dehiwala 1985

Monk on the Seashore at Dehiwala was painted during the last decade of Ivan Peries's life, which saw a return to his earlier artistic phases. This work specifically revisits his body of work from the 1960s, depicting the littoral of his birthplace, Ceylon (now Sri Lanka). Here, the figurative elements – a monk and a hut on a beach – are pushed to their greatest degree of simplicity, and the colour palette is likewise radically pared back. The artist creates texture by applying thin paint over a carefully prepared gesso ground. The work's combination of local Sri Lankan subject matter with an international modernist vocabulary carried forward a style the artist developed in the context of Ceylonese modernism in the 1930s and 1940s: Peries was one of the founding members of the '43 Group, which, as art historian Larry D. Lutchmansingh describes, 'attempted "synthesis" of the Western modern and the local non-modern, the complicating effect of the collusion between modernism and colonialism, and the effort to forge an aesthetic for a newly independent democracy'.[45] The retrospective dimension of the work gives this synthesis a further, personal inflection: in its figurative elements, *Monk on the Seashore at Dehiwala* gestures to Peries's past (a memorable experience for the artist was his convalescence from illness with a Buddhist monk) and to his desired future (he wrote of his wish to 'spend my last years in Ceylon . . . If I ever did I shall . . . live in a little hut by the sea').[46] At the same time, the painting might also represent a coastline closer to home: Southend-on-Sea, where the artist had lived since 1963 (all the while continuously contributing to the contemporary art culture of his native country). Perhaps what Peries presents to us is the grainy texture, the bright flashes of a half-imagined landscape between the places of origin and settlement.

Oil paint on board
61 x 50

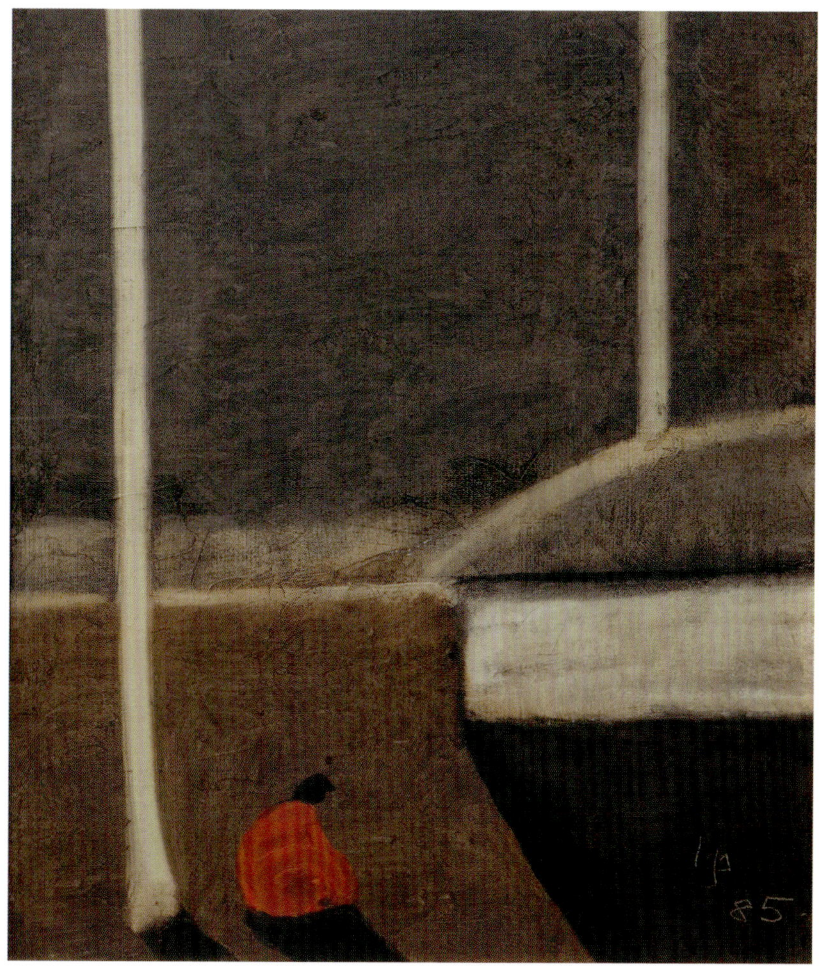

Poulomi Desai b.1965
In the Box Room 1985, digitally manipulated 1992

Alongside her extensive community work, Poulomi Desai's solo artistic practice has encompassed sound, live art and, to the greatest extent, photography. Having taught herself photography in a darkroom at Southall Youth Movement, she gave workshops as part of Autograph, an independent photography organisation associated with the British Black Arts Movement, and co-produced, with Parminder Sekhon (see p.149), the artists' book *Red Threads* 2003, exploring South Asian queer identity through photography. *In the Box Room* depicts a pair of shoes choosing between identity categories, literally concretised as boxes. Akin perhaps to Roshini Kempadoo's *Identity in Production* (see p.101), it articulates Desai's refusal to choose between parsed ethnic, sexual and gender identities. The work can also be read in the light of a comment made by Desai in an interview with Sunil Gupta (see p.79): 'The first time I met you, Pratibha Parmar introduced me to you and said, "This is Poulomi, she won't fit herself into a box, she does not call herself black, she does not call herself a woman, she does not call herself Asian, she does not call herself a lesbian . . .". I was this little young thing at this grown-up party with all these artists and I thought, how cool.'[47] In this way, Desai's photograph can be read not only for its rejection of imposed identity categories, but also for its affirmation of critical – in this case, pluralist – identities forged in the context of oppositional spaces, in conversation with comrades, mentors and elders.

35mm negative film and C-type print
Dimensions variable

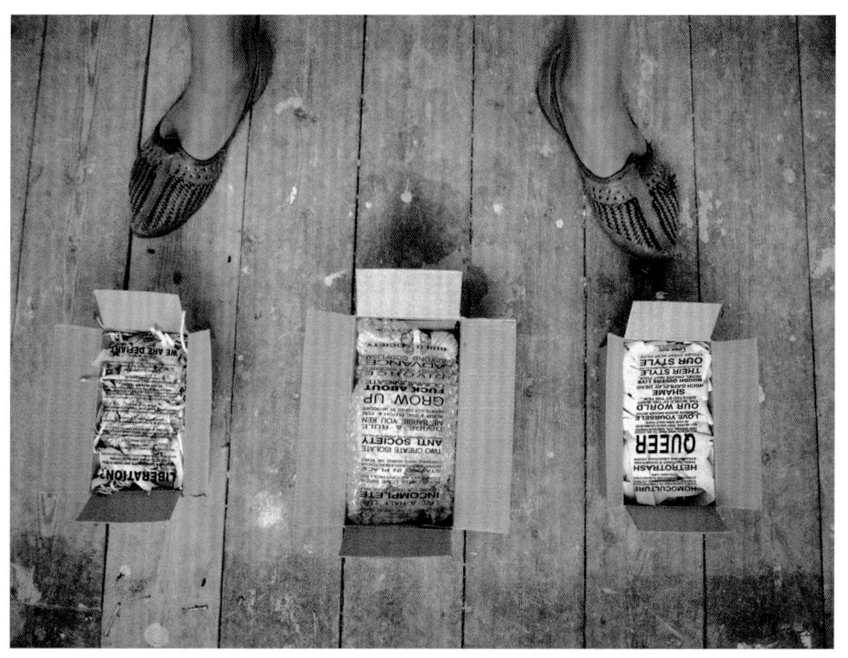

WE ARE DEFIANT
LIBERATION?
GROW UP
FUCK ABOUT
ADVANCE
ANTI SOCIETY
TWO CREATE ISOLATE
INCOMPLETE
QUEER
OUR STYLE
THEIR STYLE
SHAME
OUR WORLD
LOVE YOURSELF
HETROTRASH
HOMOCULTURE

Nina Edge b.1962
Snakes and Ladders 1985, remade 2023

Nina Edge made *Snakes and Ladders* for the *Blackwomen's Creativity Project* exhibition at the People's Gallery, London. The installation comprises a large wall-mounted batik in the background, and, in the foreground, both a ceramic breast suspended from the ceiling and two ceramic pots displayed on plinths. The work displays how a South Asian woman living in 1980s Britain had to navigate the difficulties of life structured by race, gender and class: the batik depicts a South Asian woman teetering on a precarious ladder, looking over her shoulder, surrounded by snakes which seem to be both accomplices and threats. Yet it also conveys South Asian women's everyday acts of agility in navigating these oppressive conditions, and as part of collectives: the snake to the figure's right bears the same black skin and protruding, red tongue as the goddess Kali, the symbol of South Asian feminist activism. In this sense, the installation seems to embrace the ethos of the curator of the *Blackwomen's Creativity Project* exhibition, Maud Sulter, who argued elsewhere that 'in presenting images of ourselves we affirm our worth.'[48] What is more, the work itself is an act of stealth, full of cross-cultural puns (such as 'ladies' fingers', a popular name for bhindi or okra) that play with the typical gallery-goer, ensnaring them in a web of wordplay. In keeping with the *Blackwomen's Creativity Project*, the work also intervenes against patriarchy and racism in the art world: wall-mounting a colossal batik raises the status of this medium that was denigrated at the time as 'ethnic art', while the display of ceramics on plinths overturns the inferiorisation of this medium (often practised by women), through its designation as 'craft'. *Snakes and Ladders* is a testament to, and example of, South Asian women's handicraft and sleights of hand.

Batik on paper mounted on board, ceramics, string, wooden plinths, printed text on paper, laminated
Overall display dimensions variable

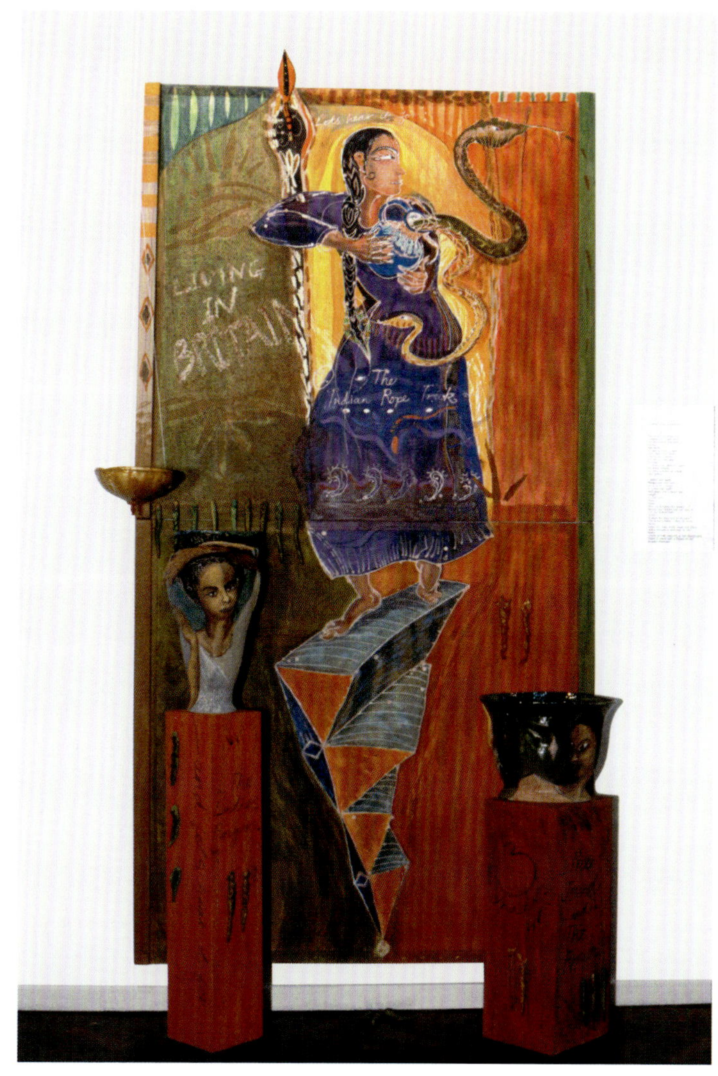
Let's hear it for
LIVING
IN
BRITAIN
The
Indian Rope Trick

Ruhul Amin b.1958
A Kind of English 1986

Ruhul Amin is a filmmaker whose work concentrates, in his words, on 'exploring the various aspects of human life, particularly that of the Asian migrant community [in Britain]'.[49] *A Kind of English* was Amin's first feature-length film, and speaks to this concern with both particular and universal aspects of human life. It depicts an East End, Sylheti Bangladeshi family (such as Amin's) building a life in conditions of diaspora, labour exploitation and racist attacks. The central character, nine-year-old Samir, symbolically poses the question of the future, while around him, his grandmother, Shahanara, and mother, Mariom, materially and emotionally sustain the home. His father, Chan, declines by dwelling in nostalgia, while his young uncle, Tariq, adopts a more empowering, hybrid, British Bangladeshi identity. Woven throughout the film is the symbolically rich narrative of Samir and his grandmother reconstructing their home in Bangladesh from rubbish gleaned from the streets of east London – but not without a Bengal tiger figurine, which attests to the element of fantasy in recalling 'home' from the vantage of diaspora. The influences of Bengali and Italian neo-realist cinema on *A Kind of English* include its inclusion of non-professional actors and its suffusion of a realist aesthetic with elements of dream and fantasy. These imagistic dimensions of Amin's work find a powerful description in the words of sociologist Sarita Malik, who speaks of Amin's '[manipulating] cinematic language – the fusing of rich, lingering images with the intensity of silence. Often little is said but within "everything else", he manages to evoke a sense of the passions which burn beneath the despair of living within this "cold climate".'[50]

Production still
16mm film 73 min

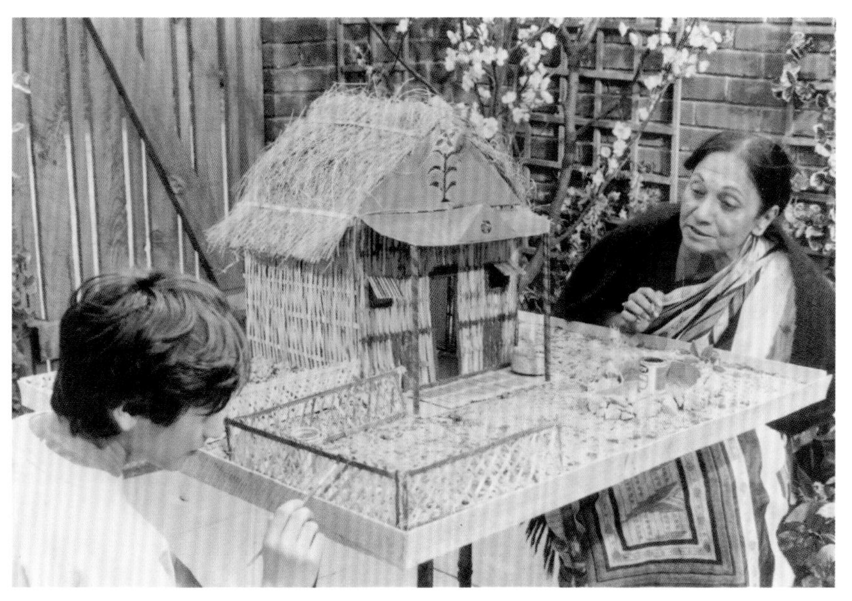

Avtarjeet Singh Dhanjal 1940–2025
Dunstall Henge 1986

Dunstall Henge is a public sculpture on Francis Green, Wolverhampton. According to dramatist and art historian Brian McAvera, this main section originally comprised 'a colonnaded entrance, planted with creepers … entered through a series of semi-circular steps and funnelling into an archway which in turn [led] into a circular space surrounded by seats cut into York stone. This space also [contained] a tall "window" and a semi-circular wall which [echoed] the semi-circular mound in the distance.'[51] Avtarjeet Dhanjal recalls taking on the work as part of a shift from making sculptures intended for display on pedestals towards a public sculpture that might '[have] its roots in that particular piece of land where it stands', and in its social geography,[52] a concern that feeds Dhanjal's broader enquiry into alienation from the natural environment, as well as alternative ecological cultures. By combining foliage, stone, concrete and steel, *Dunstall Henge* cites Dhanjal's early sculptures, in which natural matter was interlocked with industrial materials. Dhanjal undertook this early enquiry into the ecological implications of industrialisation in Punjab's post-independence capital, Chandigarh, a city famous for its modernist urban plan, and where he attended art school in the 1960s. At the same time, *Dunstall Henge* incorporates steel, one of Wolverhampton's main industries until the closure of the last foundry in 1979, thereby drawing in the work's contemporary contexts of deindustrialisation and the disenfranchisement of white and immigrant working-class constituencies in the former imperial metropole during the 1970s and 1980s. *Dunstall Henge* might therefore be understood as a critique of the long and transversal history of imperialism and industrial capitalism, made through the provision of an alternative experience of modern infrastructure and the natural landscape, one defined by localism, slowness and contemplation.

Steel, concrete aggregate and York stone
Height 400

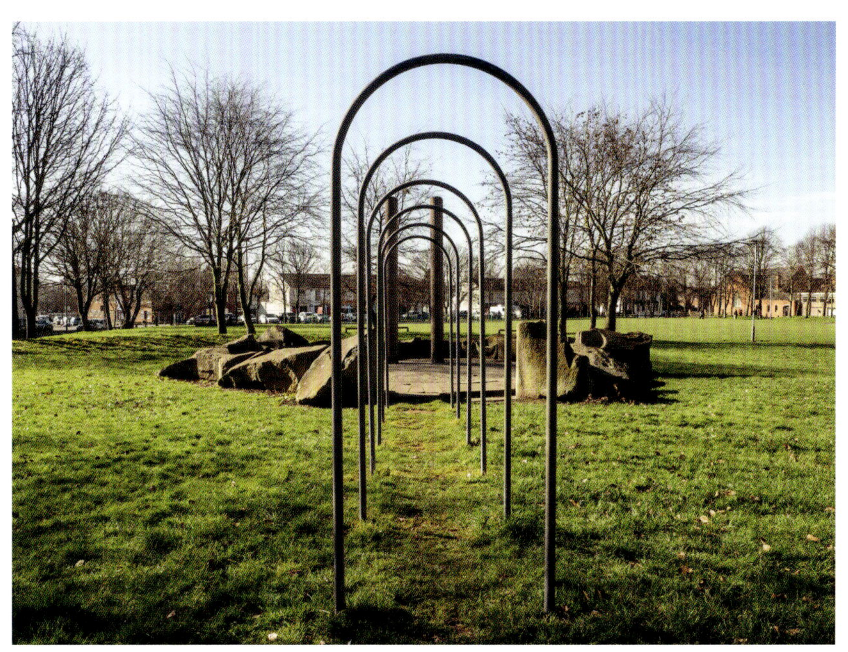

Sunil Gupta b.1953
Gay from the series *Reflections of the Black Experience* 1986

Gay, from the series *Reflections of the Black Experience*, depicts Sunil
Gupta and his then partner, Stephen Dodd, Gupta with his hands placed
protectively around Dodd's shoulders, stood in front of the entrance to
a cinema showing Hanif Kureishi's and Stephen Frears's film *My Beautiful
Laundrette* 1985, as advertised on the marquee. The cinematic reference
serves as the literal backdrop for the exploration of gay, intercultural
relationships in Gupta's depiction of the two figures: *My Beautiful Laundrette*
follows Omar (a British Pakistani entrepreneur) and Johnny (a white
working-class punk) as they explore their sexual chemistry in the context of
the violent policing of boundaries of race and sexuality in 1980s Britain. The
film's intervention has been variously analysed as offering a utopian vision of
queer, a-racial union or, for literary scholar Vinh Nguyen, as advancing a form
of multiculturalism which 'makes room for the possibility of connection and
contact, however fraught and tenuous, without denying histories of racial
violence or flattening out forms of difference'.[53] Gupta's portrait of himself
and his partner represents a personal experience of the same moment:
the pressures of racialisation, for instance, are conveyed via Dodd's pale
attire and Gupta's dark attire, while the potential fraughtness of a queer
intercultural relationship is suggested by the figures' stance – intimate but
also tentative and protective. At the same time, the reference to the film
affirms that the difficult navigation of queer intercultural romantic life,
captured in the self-portrait, was not happening in isolation, but as part of a
broader culture and as a collective endeavour in 1980s Britain.

Photograph, gelatin silver print on paper
28.7 x 19.1

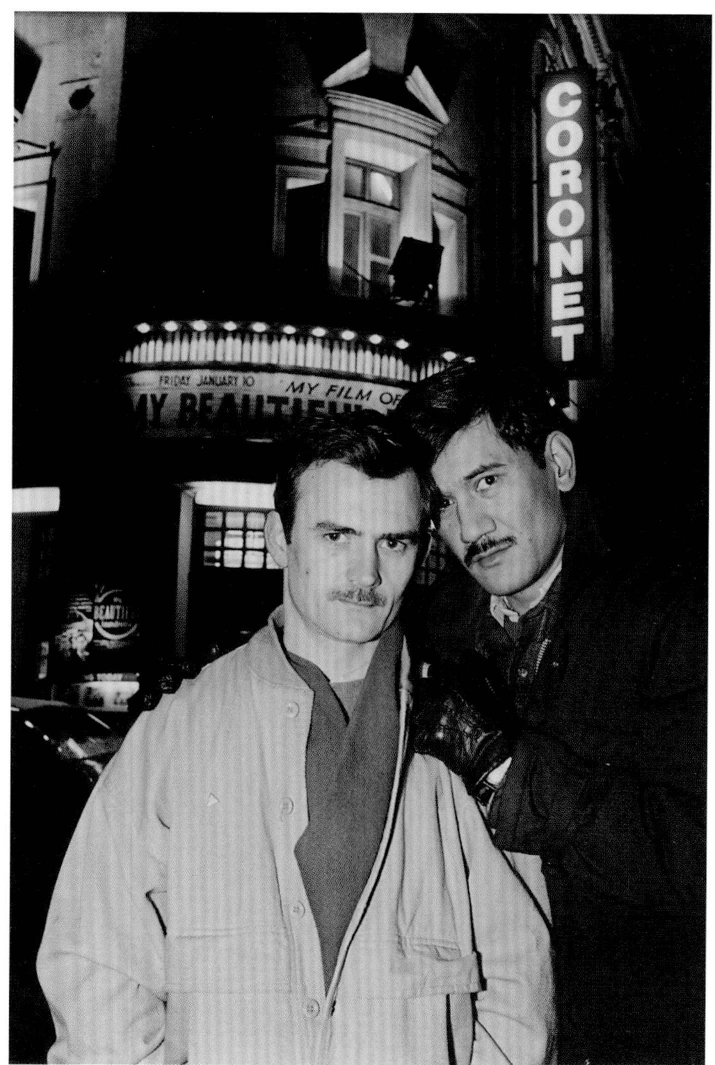

CORONET
FRIDAY JANUARY 10   MY FILM OF
MY BEAUTIFUL

Pratibha Parmar b.1955
Emergence 1986

Emergence is an experimental documentary on the British Black Arts
Movement, specifically its feminist current, as seen from within. It portrays
how this inaugural generation with roots in the formerly colonised world, yet
born and raised in Britain, were, as the voiceover tells us, 'rising, rising, rising.
From yesterday's silence to tomorrow's dreams.' The film depicts works
produced in this context, such as Sutapa Biswas's *Housewives with Steak-
Knives* 1983–5 (p.59). It reproduces footage of Mona Hatoum's performance
artwork *Under Siege* 1982, the artist confined in a box made of wood and
plastic sheeting, helplessly slipping in mud before getting up and falling
down again. In Hatoum's commentary, she tells us that the work draws on
'the bloody history of [her] own [Palestinian] people' to make 'a statement
about a persistent state of struggle to survive in a continuous state of
siege'. Another figure Parmar profiles is the poet Meiling Jin, who gives a
reading on her family history of Chinese indentureship in the Caribbean.
Clearly, Parmar herself is part of the movement depicted – not least as she
includes footage of the film playing on a monitor. Beyond documenting the
movement as it was emerging, Parmar also uses montage – the technique
of selecting, editing and piecing together separate sections of film to form
a continuous whole – to represent its unified yet unwieldy structure, as
it was later described by artist Lubaina Himid: 'We were . . . a fluid set of
women who were not prepared to be herded into a single way of expressing
ourselves.'[54] Following historian Mahmood Mamdani's assertion that activist
groups are test spaces for new societies, the sociality of anti-racist feminist
artists, which Parmar translates into filmic form in *Emergence*, might be
taken to be a precursor for multicultural social reorganisation at large.[55]

Colour VHS
18 min

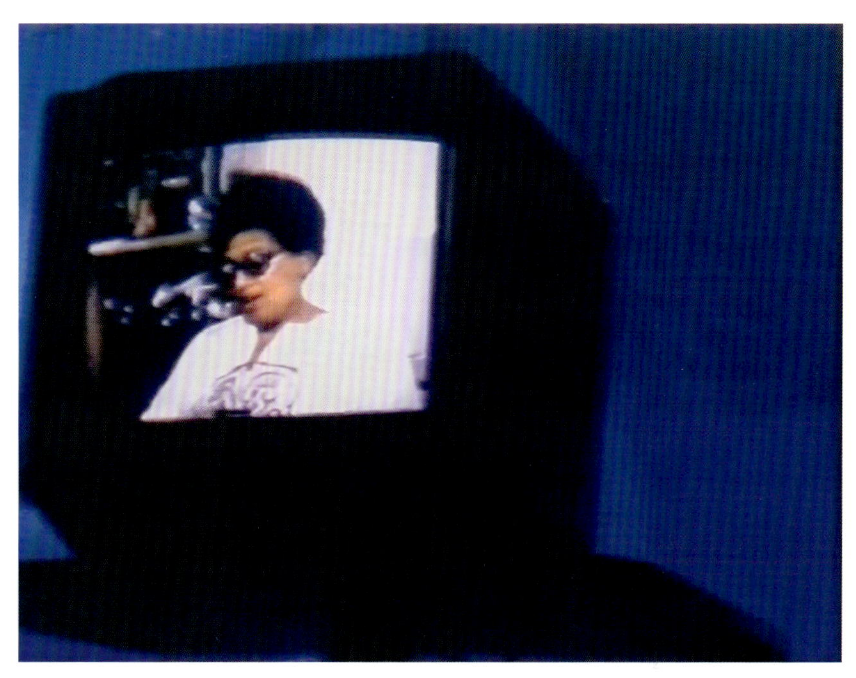

Molly Shinhat b.1964
Molly Shinhat (self-portrait), Montreal, Canada 1986
from the series *I'm the problem, I'm not white* 1986

Molly Shinhat was born in 1964 in Wolverhampton, a centre of racist antagonisms and anti-racist resistance – Enoch Powell, known for his brazenly racist populism, was her family's MP – before her family moved to Montreal in 1976. In 1986, Shinhat was travelling from New Delhi to Montreal via London on an Indian passport, and was told by border officials she had to apply for a British visa, even though she had joint British citizenship. At this moment, she decided to pause her studies and spend an extended period in London. She recalls this act as one of defiance, intended to 'show Thatcher, who was intensifying Britain's racialised border regime, that [she] could, and to join in with anti-racist organising in Britain at the time'.[56] In London, Shinhat contributed to socialist, anti-racist and feminist photography cultures; for instance, she was part of the collective that produced *Polareyes: A Journal by and About Black Women Working in Photography* 1987. *I'm the problem, I'm not white* is part of a series made in Canada, consisting of pairs of images superimposed in camera (Shinhat shot once underexposed, then shot again on the same film), and was subsequently used as the cover image of the first and only issue of *Polareyes*. It consists of a self-portrait of the artist looking directly at the viewer, and partially blocking her face with her forearms: at once an act of claiming agency and of defence. This is superimposed with the context of this dual gesture: a spectral image of a veiled and bejewelled bride, a stereotype of South Asian femininity, but perhaps also a representation of the possibility of cultural reclamation. In such ways, Shinhat's technical experimentation hardwires representational complexity in the medium of photography.

Kodak 100 colour negative film
27.9 x 35.6

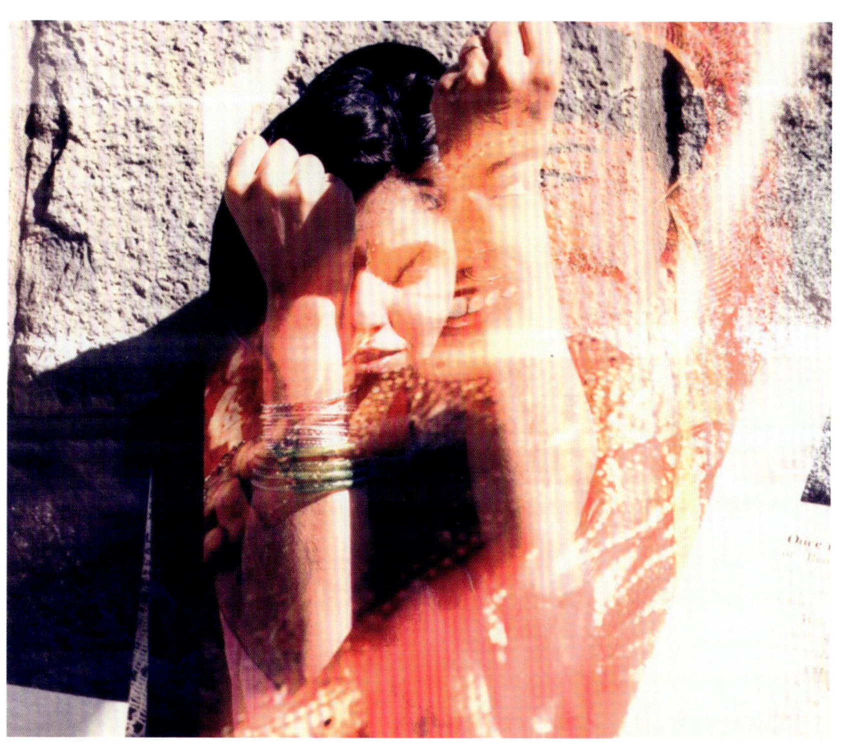

Zarina Bhimji b.1963
She Loved to Breathe – Pure Silence 1987

This panel from the installation work *She Loved to Breathe – Pure Silence*
consists of muslin cloth squashed between two square panes of Perspex.[57]
One side, reproduced here, bears a poem, along with a pair of furled latex
gloves.[58] In preparation for making the artwork, Zarina Bhimji interviewed
South Asian women who worked at Heathrow Airport; her poem conveys
their experiences of drudgery and precarity, their subjection to racist abuse,
their capability in defending themselves and their bonds of sisterhood.
Meanwhile, the latex gloves evoke sensory memories of the smell and touch
of this staple piece of equipment for various kinds of care work – labour
that is often undertaken by migrant women. Critics including Mark Haworth-
Booth have also linked the way in which the gloves seem to probe folds of
muslin 'skin' to the invasiveness of 'virginity tests', which formed a rallying
point for South Asian feminist activists, including Bhimji, at the time.[59]
Her use of muslin summons tactile memories of the softness of a baby's
swaddle, but also invokes the use of the same material as a burial garment
in the Ismaili Islamic tradition into which Bhimji was born. Altogether, the
work stages an encounter between the viewer and the simultaneously
racialised, gendered and classed experiences of British South Asian women
at the most intimate levels: psychic cornerstones (infancy and death) and
the body (appealing to sight, touch, smell and, via the voices in the poem,
sound). As several scholars have pointed out, this is how Bhimji offers a
contribution to social transformation: in art historian Allison Young's words,
the work '[expands] our capacity to imagine others'.[60]

Detail comprising muslin, Letraset, latex gloves and Perspex
49.7 x 51 x 1.2

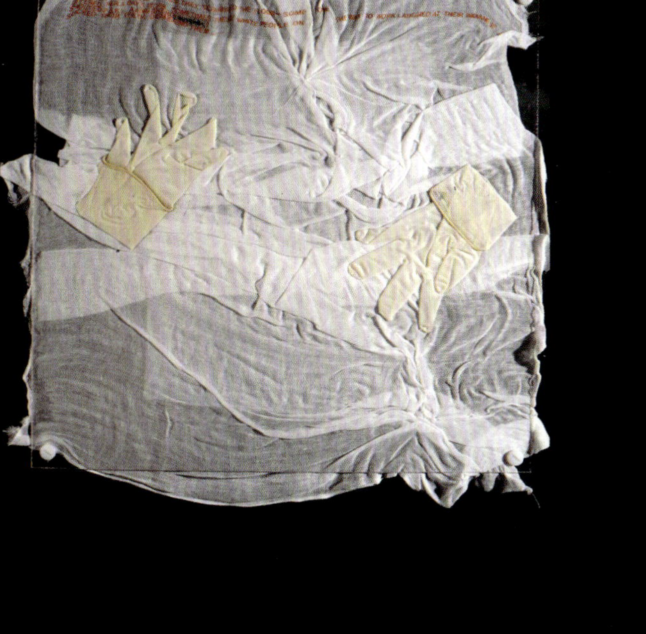

Sardul Gill b.1938
Earth Shrine 1987

This work, from Sardul Gill's *Earth Shrine* series, comprises a photograph
of a picture frame demarcating a patch of rubbish-strewn land, within
which the artist has assembled a subtle composition of organic matter,
discarded objects retrieved from a skip, and mounds of bright pigment. This
photograph is presented to the viewer within a picture frame (the same one
used in the photograph itself). The series title alludes to wayside shrines
in India, specifically pitha: rectangular enclosures of white-washed mud-
bricks, where locals and passers-by make offerings to the Goddess.[61] Gill's
work clearly alludes to pitha, yet the artist adds an ecological dimension:
the baking of synthetic objects into the land, and the sprouting of plant life,
call attention to interactions between man-made detritus and the natural
environment over time. In ways that parallel Avtarjeet Dhanjal's *Dunstall
Henge* (p.77), Gill's social, spiritual and ecological work might be read in
the context of the contemporary decline of cities such as Nottingham
– where he has lived since 1970, having arrived in Britain from Punjab via
Nairobi in 1963. Indeed, the work's incorporation of discarded materials
evokes the widespread rendering of people and materials as so much waste
during deindustrialisation and the transformation to an economy based
on services and finance, centred in London and the south-east of England.
Within this moment, *Earth Shrine* kindles a renewed spiritual and ecological
consciousness, as well as a commitment to localism, as exemplified by the
wayside shrines, which recognise where a community assigns value within its
own locality.

Drawing with powder colours into soil with discarded
objects embedded, defined by a dilapidated picture frame
47.5 × 57.5

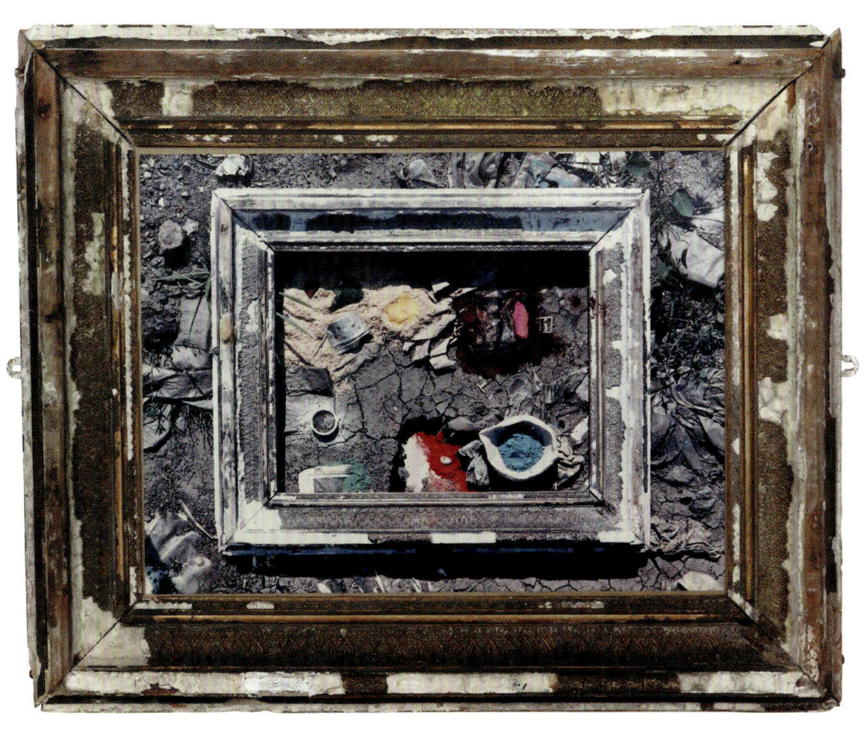

Mumtaz Karimjee b.1950
In Search of an Image 1987

In Search of an Image comprises an arrangement of black-and-white photographic self-portraits of the artist along with fragments of text, cumulatively drawing out a reflection on the external projection of racial and/or sexual otherness in Western and South Asian cultures, and the Muslim, South Asian, lesbian woman's struggle for self-actualisation. Titled 'The Eastern Disease?', a vertical panel on the left addresses the historical European projection of sexual deviancy onto the colonised world. In a descending sequence of three images, the artist first adopts the role of the alluring, Eastern woman from Orientalist paintings, before reversing roles, becoming the European male spectator, complete with glasses, a tobacco pipe and an empowered gaze looking back at the camera. The identically structured panel on the right, titled 'The Western Disease?', concerns the prohibition on homosexuality through its identifications as a 'Western disease' in South Asian settings, in the context of its contestation by South Asian, lesbian and feminist activism. This panel first consists of an image of Mumtaz Karimjee looking downcast, behind a row of incense sticks and candles – perhaps a gesture of tribute to South Asian women killed for having compromised their families' 'honour' – alongside a short confessional text about the artist's experience of feeling burdened and threatened by the concept of honour. Next, a politicised Karimjee looks up, defiant and resolute (an image paired with a galvanising quote by feminist theorist Gloria Anzaldúa). The third photo is an act of movement-building, whereby the artist invites the viewer to read and draw their own conclusions from an article on the dismissal of two women police officers in India for marrying one other. In the centre of these two panels is a single photograph of the artist crouched beneath a tree, resembling a seed: a symbol, perhaps, of the act of regenerating her own identity. *In Search of an Image* stages the struggles of a South Asian lesbian woman to extricate herself from the overdeterminations of Eastern and Western cultural and sexual discourses, and to carve out her own space alongside her sisters. In keeping with the leftist photography cultures in which Karimjee was involved at the time, which understood visual representation and social realities as co-constitutive, this search for autonomy is rendered as a 'search for an image'.

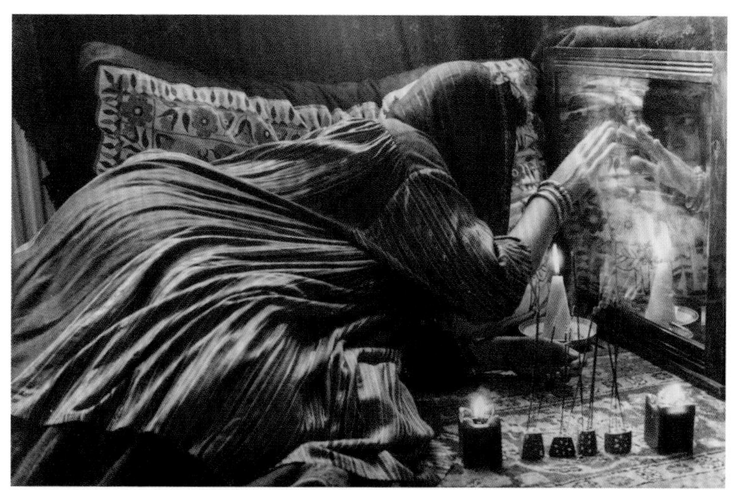

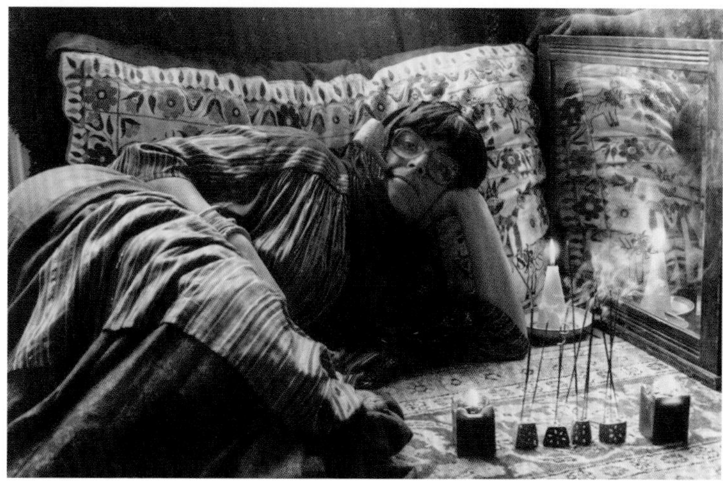

2 of 13 framed photographs and printed text
Overall display 111.1 x 111.1

Shaheen Merali b.1959
Unilever Strike 1987

Unilever Strike is a large batik based on a photograph, perhaps from a newspaper or magazine, of security guards who had been fired from Hindustan Lever (the Indian subsidiary of Unilever) in 1986 for demanding pay rises in line with India's Minimum Wages Act. The work depicts the men on the picket line displaying banners communicating their struggle to the viewer, including the line, 'We are the security workmen of "Hindustan Lever" who have been thrown on the street'. As such, it indicates the necessity of supporting the Indian workers' struggle to British activists, through immediately comprehensible social connections – Unilever is a consumer goods giant – as well as through deeper historical ties. Unilever originated in the British soap company Lever Brothers, which was enabled by colonial expansion to extract palm oil as a central ingredient in its lucrative industrial soap-making process. In 1931, an Indian subsidiary was set up to produce and monopolise an Indian market for household goods. Moreover, Shaheen Merali's choice of medium, batik, attests to a parallel history of unequal, trans-local circuits of exchange: batik originated in Indonesia before becoming industrialised by Dutch and then British colonisers, who exported the fabric from factories in the metropole to colonial markets. The case made for trans-local, anti-racist, anti-colonial solidarities in *Unilever Strike* can be understood in the context of the British Black Arts Movement. It also speaks to the work's immediate moment of the renewal of internationalist cultural and social network models – as at the Tercera Bienal de la Habana 1989, a well-known Third Worldist art biennial in Cuba, where Merali co-facilitated the exhibition of works by contemporary artists from Britain, and showed *Unilever Strike* – on the cusp of a historical shift that would see the end of the Cold War and the rapid globalisation of neoliberal capitalism.

Batik on cotton

150 × 200

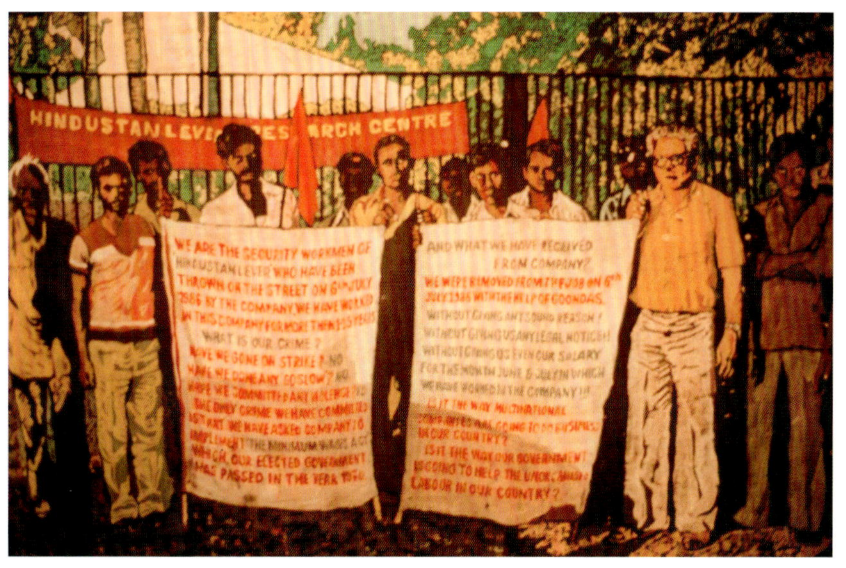

HINDUSTAN LEVER RESEARCH CENTRE
WE ARE THE SECURITY WORKMEN OF 'HINDUSTAN LEVER LTD' WHO HAVE BEEN THROWN ON THE STREET ON 6th JULY 1986 BY THE COMPANY, WE HAVE WORKED IN THIS COMPANY FOR MORE THAN 15 YEARS
WHAT IS OUR CRIME?
HAVE WE GONE ON STRIKE? NO
HAVE WE DONE ANY GO SLOW? NO
HAVE WE COMMITTED ANY VIOLENCE? NO
THE ONLY CRIME WE HAVE COMMITTED IS THAT WE HAVE ASKED COMPANY TO IMPLEMENT THE MINIMUM WAGES ACT WHICH OUR ELECTED GOVERNMENT HAS PASSED IN THE VERA YEAR.
AND WHAT WE HAVE RECEIVED FROM COMPANY?
WE WERE REMOVED FROM THE JOB ON 6th JULY 1986 WITH THE HELP OF GOONDAS.
WITHOUT GIVING ANY SOUND REASON!
WITHOUT GIVING US ANY LEGAL NOTICE!!
WITHOUT GIVING US EVEN OUR SALARY FOR THE MONTH JUNE & JULY IN WHICH WE HAVE WORKED IN THE COMPANY!!!
IS IT THE WAY MULTINATIONAL COMPANIES WILL GOING TO DO BUSINESS IN OUR COUNTRY?
IS IT THE WAY OUR GOVERNMENT IS GOING TO HELP THE BLACK LABOUR IN OUR COUNTRY?

Amal Ghosh 1933–2022
Flight II 1989

Flight II depicts a dynamic configuration of forms – two horses; a woman in a yellow robe astride one of the horses; a half-human, half-bird creature; a reclining nude, impossibly lying flat on the horse's flank; and a bald figure grasping at the others – against a flat, red background. The work exhibits some of the key features of Amal Ghosh's practice, as identified by critic and filmmaker Sonali Fernando: the representation of 'shards of different myths', from varying cultural sources, that 'jostle together', and the '[yielding of] his fabular narrative . . . to a hidden language of colour, space and form'.[62] As indicated by the title, this painting concerns flight: the horses are at a canter, and the figures lurch towards the canvas's edge, creating a forward trajectory across the painting. Meanwhile, the symbols and 'shards of different myths' in this work pertain to stories of flight: the bird is the quintessential symbol of migration, while the motif of a figure on a horse calls to mind any number of references, not least the flight of Joseph, Mary, and the infant Jesus into Egypt (allowing for an association between Ghosh's horse and the donkey of the New Testament story). There are also counterforces to flight in the work, including the figure on the right, whose oversized hands attempt to claw back the central figures, and the impossibly placed figurative elements, which equally fix the composition in stasis. Moreover, there is no background context in the work – notably, no sense of where the flight is from, or where it is directed towards. This is therefore a painting focused on flight itself, on intransitive flight, an act conceived of as comprising a tension between propulsion and resistance, and one that we might expect to have interested an artist who lived a peripatetic existence between India and Britain.

Oil paint on canvas
183 × 143

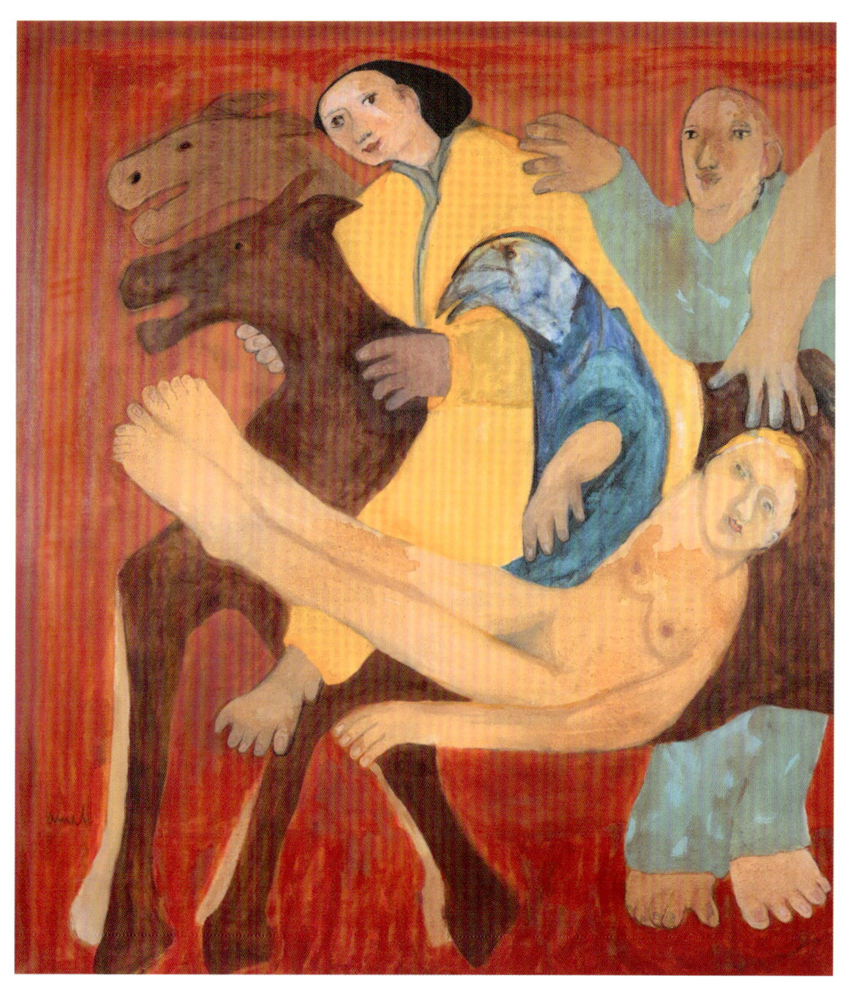

Said Adrus b.1958
Portrait of Another Kind 1990

Said Adrus's body of work from the 1980s explores the relation between the grand
claims of state institutions – such as appeals to justice and the rule of law – and the
lived experiences of diasporic communities. Within this broader corpus, *Portrait of
Another Kind* is a notably private, expressive work. It focuses on the tension between
state discourses of identity and belonging, and the diasporic subject's identity
formation. The work comprises a faceless figure flailing behind British passport
insignia, affixed to the painted surface with strips of fabric. This configuration might
be read as an indictment of the notion that official identities can suture the exilic
subject's sense of self – notwithstanding the privileges they can provide – and indeed
as a recognition of the participation of postcolonial state institutions (including, but
not limited to, the British state) in the material dislocations that render coherent
identity formation impossible for swathes of people in the modern era. The figure –
suspended in a blue expanse evoking the quintessential migratory spaces of the sea
and the sky – is hopelessly disoriented. Adrus diminishes the figure's feet, recalling
postcolonial theorist Edward Said's reflection that 'the pathos of exile is in the loss
of contact with the solidity and satisfaction of earth'.[63] By exploring the question of
identity-building in the context of nationalisms, Adrus confronts some of the legacies
of empire and independent nation-state formation – including Ugandan South Asian
statelessness in the 1970s, which the artist personally experienced[64] – while also
cautioning against their repetition in the work's present historical moment, when
the prelude to the formation of the European Union in 1992 saw the emergence
of a 'white continentalism'.[65] Simultaneously, around the edges of the work, Adrus
repeatedly writes the phrase 'Ain't Ethnic Art', rebuking the depoliticisation of
artworks such as *Portrait of Another Kind* through their categorisation as 'ethnic art'
within the liberal-multiculturalist cultural sector (as discussed in the introduction).

Oil paint and mixed media on two canvases
166 x 71

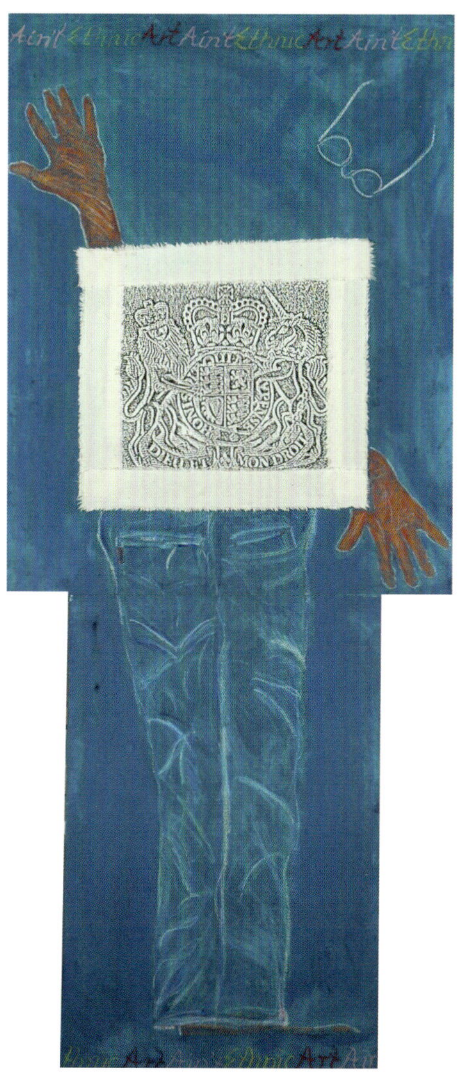

Ain't Ethnic Art Ain't Ethnic Art Ain't Ethni

Hamad Butt 1962–94
Transmission 1990

Transmission is a sculpture comprising a circle of nine glass books resting on metal stands, each connected by electrical cabling and emitting UV light. Etched into the glass of each book is an image of a Triffid, the carnivorous plant in John Wyndham's science fiction novel *The Day of the Triffids* 1951 which blinds and eats humans. As the viewer moves around the circle, the image flits in and out of visibility. In the work's original exhibition as part of Hamad Butt's degree show at Goldsmiths' College, London, in 1990, there was also a glass vitrine containing hatching and perishing flies. The title – read in conjunction with Butt's contemporary essays, written from a British Pakistani and HIV-positive standpoint – draws relations between the work and multiple forms of 'transmission'. On the one hand, the work's sensory intensity, and indeed the dying flies in the work's initial exhibition, suggest the trauma experienced by the queer community during the AIDS epidemic. On the other hand, the discursive 'transmissions' engaged by the work include the structural homophobia of medical institutions during the AIDS epidemic, which Butt linked to their historical entanglement with race science during the colonial period, as well as contemporary nationalist articulations of religious knowledge.[66] In relation to these epistemological disseminations, *Transmission* hones in on the dualism of visibility and invisibility. For instance, the emission of UV light (i.e., the invisible light in all light) suggests an invisibility within the project of enlightenment, including modern science. Oscillation between visibility and invisibility might indeed be identified as Butt's response to the AIDS epidemic, the aftermath of colonialism, and nationalism: a representational gesture whereby opening oneself up mentally and corporeally to the other's vision, and acknowledging the inevitable partialness of such an exchange, are of equal ethical necessity.

Glass, steel, ultraviolet lights and electrical cables
Overall display dimensions variable

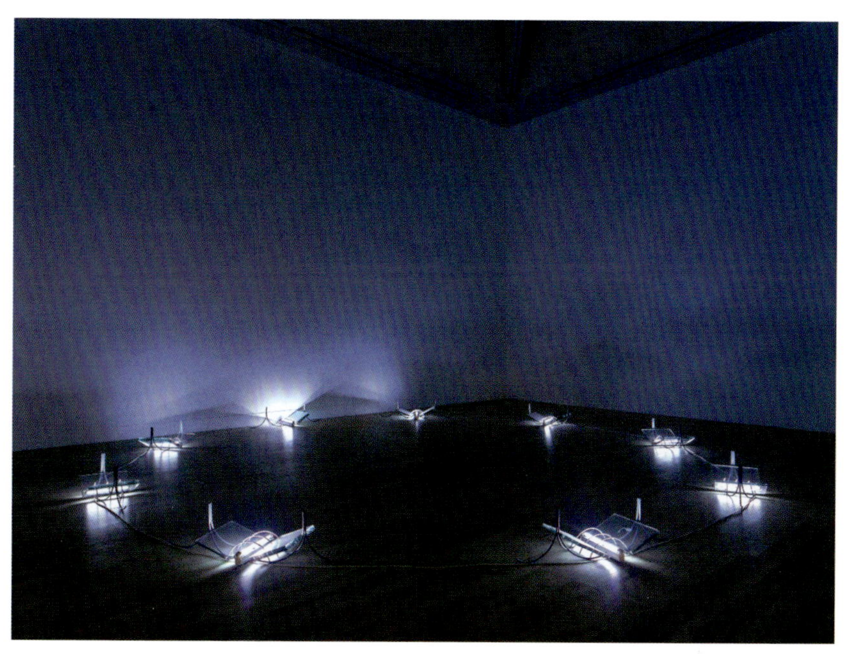

Al-An deSouza b.1958
Spit and Polish 1990

Spit and Polish depicts two floating, intertwined figures, one of them winged.[67] They are either wrestling or engaging in a sexual act; their facial expressions and body language indeterminately suggest pleasure or pain. The coupled figures quote Salman Rushdie's two archetypes of postcolonial migrants in *The Satanic Verses*: Gibreel Farishta ('Angel Gabriel', a film star who sings his loyalty to Indian nationalism), and Saladin Chamcha (a proud Anglophile), who, in the opening of the novel, are clutched in such a tight embrace that Chamcha feels 'metamorphic, hybrid, as if he were growing into the person whose head nestled now between his legs'.[68] At the same time, Al-An deSouza's work draws on research of their South Asian heritage; for instance, against a background of wallpaper with a pattern of gestating foetuses, the artist depicts four framed images relating to Portuguese colonialism in Goa. This can be read in the context of the contemporary reconstitution of oppositional political constituencies in Britain, and specifically the burgeoning of British South Asian cultural activist spaces within a broader, transcultural anti-racist collective. Within such spaces, practitioners examined the specificities of subcontinental history (as exemplified in *Spit and Polish*), as well as delineating the racialisation experienced by British South Asians. Another aspect of the work, as artist and curator Yong Soon Min points out, '[contests] simplistic notions of a fixed and binary sexual and racial construction'.[69] One of many ways in which deSouza troubles gender and racial categorisations is through their choice of medium: shoe polish and lipstick. These are, respectively, quintessentially masculine and feminine materials, and, by blending the two, deSouza performs the smudging of this duality. In all these respects, *Spit and Polish* explores the possibility that multitudes can constitute a single experience, serving as a crucible for a social ethos of pluralism.

Lipstick, shoe polish and collage
136 x 92

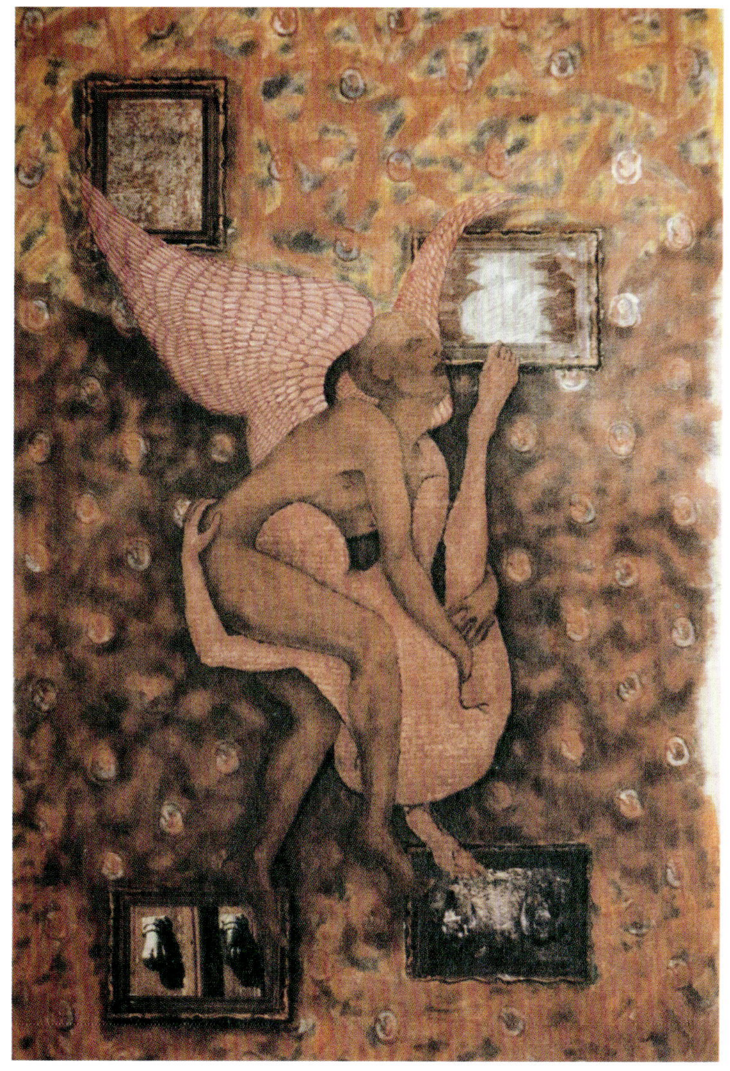

Roshini Kempadoo b.1959
Identity in Production 1990

Identity in Production pairs a black-and-white, triple-exposure photograph
of the artist, seen wearing the head coverings of the multiple cultures
encompassed in her heritage (she claims East Indian, West Indian, Amerindian
and European descent), with the text, 'Who do they expect me to be today.'
This text speaks to the friction, explored in the work, between the hybrid
identities of people with diasporic trajectories, and the narrow categories
to which they are expected to conform; as art historian Kellie Jones argues,
Identity in Production carves out a photographic space that is 'wholly inclusive'
of identities characterised by 'fragmentation and dislocation'.[70] The distinctly
political charge of the piece – two of the self-portraits confrontationally
return the viewer's gaze, refusing to be objectified, while another has her
eyes closed, perhaps in a self-protective gesture – has its roots in Marxist
and feminist photographic movements (Roshini Kempadoo was a member
of the all-women's photography agency Format), and especially in 'black'
photography. The work is also notably devoid of the conventional backgrounds
of essentialising representations (a sultry harem, perhaps, or a tropical island)
– instead, the portraits' context is black. And indeed 'black' politics: *Identity in
Production* was made for the first touring exhibition of the independent 'black'
photography organisation Autograph, which, by fostering a culture of self-
representation, contested 'black representation [in contemporary media and
culture] . . . for example, in relation to the use of the black subject as abstract
signifier of "black violence"; or as the figure of "otherness" – simultaneously
exotic and primitive, victim and villain'.[71] The contribution of *Identity in
Production* to this broader project is to refute monolithic identity categories,
by allowing three culturally specific self-portraits to coexist.

Silver gelatin print on paper
40 × 35

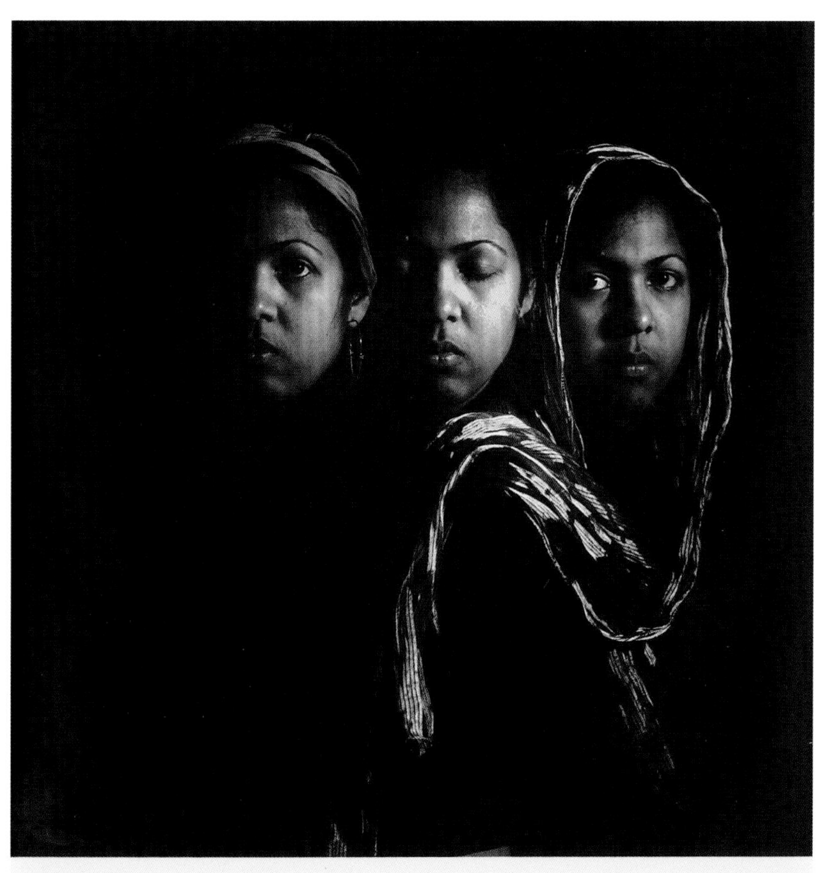

Who do they expect me to be today.

Shakila Taranum Maan b.1962
Ferdous 1990

The film *Ferdous* explores Islam from a lesbian perspective. Its loose narrative begins
with a straight wedding, presided over by an imam representing a dominant, hetero-
patriarchal Muslim culture. Yet Shakila Maan suggests that the event of marriage, around
which hetero-patriarchy is organised, is also an opportunity for female friendship and
homoeroticism that cuts against its grain: a bridal party sequence encompasses women
dancing, singing, adorning each other, in a sensuous environment replete with swathes
of fabric, tinkling jewellery and powdered skin. A soundtrack and dances reminiscent
of Sufi practices introduce a kindred Muslim culture, in which homoerotic devotional
poems were common. A later sequence shows two women relaxing and embracing in
Leighton House in London (thus, like Mumtaz Karimjee's artwork, see p.89, reclaiming
Orientalist material culture).[72] Yet none of this, Maan suggests, can overcome the power
of hetero-patriarchal Muslim cultures. After a Qur'anic verse prohibiting 'lewdness
(unnatural crimes)' rolls on-screen, a poetic sequence suggests that the wayward
bride has been detained, or worse. Such a contentious gloss of the verse suggests that
homophobia is inherent to Islam itself. This gesture can be understood in the context of
Maan's activism with Women Against Fundamentalism (WAF), a group founded in 1989
to bolster coalitions defending Salman Rushdie's *The Satanic Verses*, with the specific
aim of overturning gender and sexual injustice within hetero-patriarchal religious
cultures. Ultimately, *Ferdous* follows WAF in extending its excoriation of hetero-
patriarchy beyond self-styled Islamic regimes (Maan's film was inspired by a report of a
lesbian woman's incarceration in Iran) or dominant Islamic cultures to Islam itself. Thus,
despite its engagement with historical and contemporary queer Islamic cultures, the
film, like WAF, risks complicity with colonial discourses of Muslim backwardness and
barbarism, and its renewal since the late 1980s to vilify working-class British Muslim men
as the state's primary internal enemy.

Production still
Super 8 film 8 min

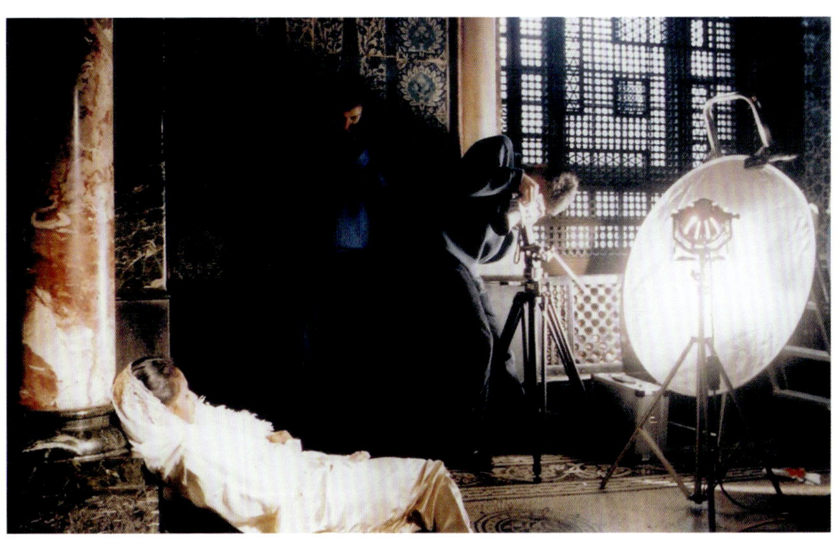

Shanti Panchal b.1951
Mannequin 1990

For art historian Deborah Swallow, Shanti Panchal's watercolour paintings
are 'both autobiographical and universal, embedded in an Indian context
and deeply spiritual in feeling, yet speaking to and of the world'.[73] *Mannequin*
perhaps speaks specifically to the fundamental question of social relationality.
It depicts a figure in the barest suggestion of a bedroom, gesturing towards
two tailor's dummies. The work bears the key features of Panchal's style
since the 1980s: a strenuously worked surface (he 'injects' watercolour into
the paper by hammering and scraping the surface and building up layers of
pigment); flatness and absence of shadows; a colour palette of earth and
blazing sunsets, which he has related to memories of his hometown, Mesar,
Gujarat; and figures that seem to be 'of the inner world rather than the
outer'.[74] Panchal had already made use of the tailor's dummy in a 1988 painting
commissioned by the Imperial War Museum in London on the production
of army uniforms. In *Mannequin*, the artist reinserts the motif of the tailor's
dummy into a painting that reflects on the relationship between the self and
the world. *Mannequin*'s unclothed figure is located between a bed (the place,
as artist Carol Mavor has pointed out, where we are born and die)[75] and a
wardrobe (where we prepare to present ourselves to others), thus in an
intermediate zone between private and public. With a poised hand that seems
to be the focal point of the painting, charged with the power of deliberation,
the figure seems to be considering the different identities they might adopt, as
represented by the dummies. While resonating with the diasporic experience
of being urged to choose between being 'eastern' or 'western', *Mannequin* also
addresses the broader question of navigating the uncertain space between
who we are and who we are impelled to be.

Watercolour on paper
79 x 98

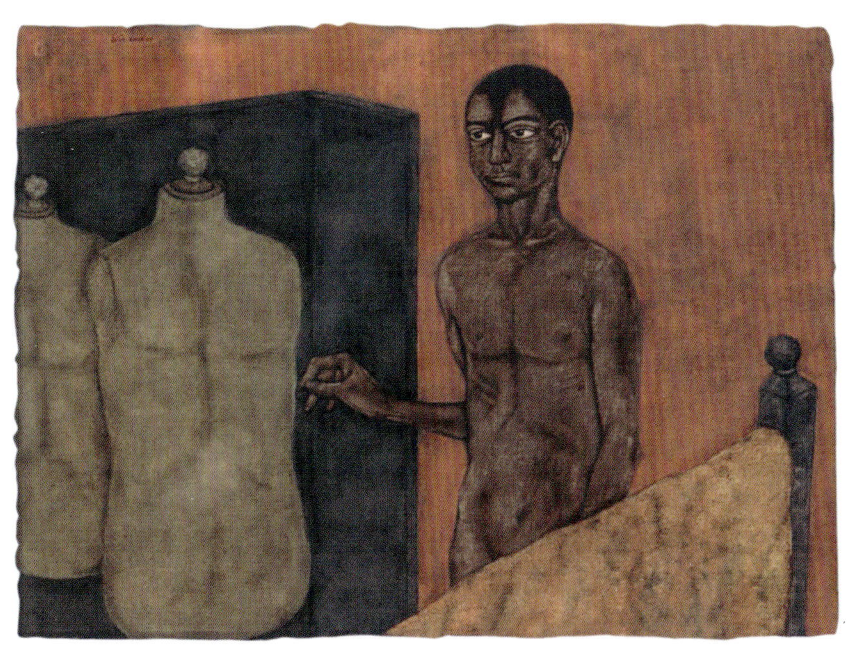

Nudrat Afza b.1955
Shop, Gibbet Street 1991

Nudrat Afza began teaching herself photography in 1986, before building
up her practice by working with community organisations. Afza has
been steadfastly committed to exploring 'the possibility of the camera
to confront the struggle to be seen and represented in daily life',[76] and
to the social context of Manningham, Bradford, which has had a strong
working-class Azad Kashmiri, and Indian and Pakistani Punjabi community
since a wave of labour migration in the 1950s and 1960s, and where Afza
has been based since migrating from Rawalpindi, Pakistan, aged nine. This
early photograph of a South Asian woman comparing the ripeness of
two bunches of turnips in a corner shop is a case in point. It exploits the
potential subversiveness of the corner shop as a social space (prevalently
owned by immigrants, and, as author and presenter Babita Sharma
writes, a site for working out social attitudes and relations 'from below')
to put forward a rare representation of a commanding and self-assured
South Asian woman.[77] Counter to racialised hierarchies of knowledge in
Western academic institutions, Afza takes seriously her subject's expertise
in evaluating the quality of turnips. Moreover, the composition, with the
figure, and foliage projecting outwards from her, filling the entire span of
the photograph, conveys a sense of her stateliness. Her absorption in her
activity stabilises the scene, momentarily stilling the hustle and bustle of the
corner shop in the background. Afza encourages the viewer to be beholden
to her subject's sense of time, and to her act of looking.

35mm colour negative film
Dimensions variable

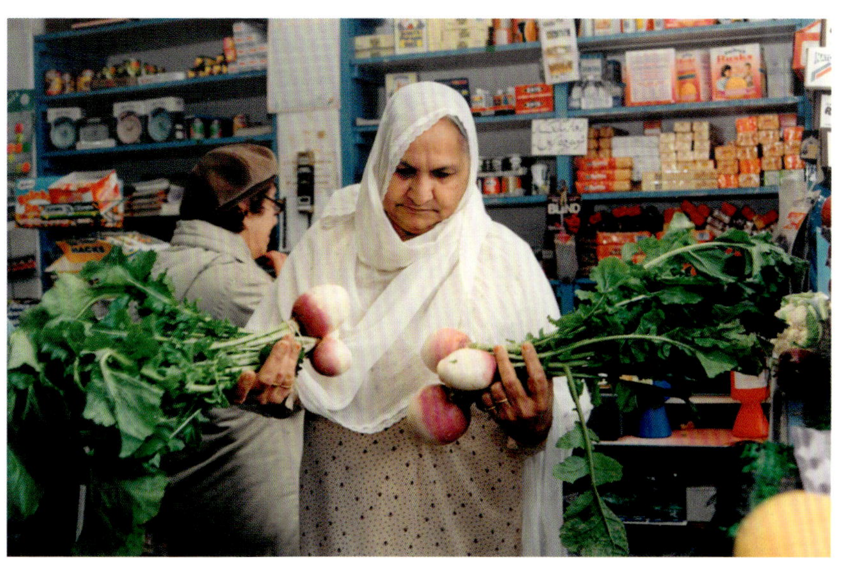

Keith Khan b.1963
Flying Costumes, Floating Tombs 1991

Flying Costumes, Floating Tombs was a performance comprising sculpture, dance, performance and sound, based on the Hosay procession which takes place each year in Trinidad, the birthplace of Keith Khan's parents. In its remembrance of the Battle of Karbala (discussed in relation to the work of Jamil Dehlavi, p.47), Hosay adapts Persian and South Asian commemorations of this historical struggle against tyranny, cultural practices that nineteenth-century indentured Indian labourers had brought to Trinidad, primarily by incorporating aspects of Carnival. For Khan, Hosay was also significant as a historical form of resistance against British colonial oppression.[78] This photograph – which depicts one of two colossal tadjahs (symbols of the Prophet's grandsons' tombs), suspended from a crane – was taken at a performance in Bristol. Out of shot is Bristol Harbour in the background, yet we can see infrastructure on the other side of the dock: Bristol Industrial Museum, and cargo cranes (by repeating this structure in his performance, Khan fastens it in the cityscape). In bringing Hosay from Trinidad to Bristol, Khan drew linkages between violence in the colonies and prosperity in the metropole in an era when the statue of Edward Colston remained standing, and Bristol's role in histories of slavery and colonialism was not yet engrained in public memory. At the same time, Khan carries vernacular cultures of anti-colonial resistance into the belly of the beast. This defiant mapping of coordinates in the face of postcolonial amnesia paralleled that of the generation to which Khan belonged as it claimed the identity 'black British', as well as that of the famous anti-racist slogan, written by activist and writer A. Sivanandan: 'We are here because you were there'.

Detail comprising ripstop nylon, fibreglass rods, steel mirrors, plywood, sequins and a crane
Dimensions variable

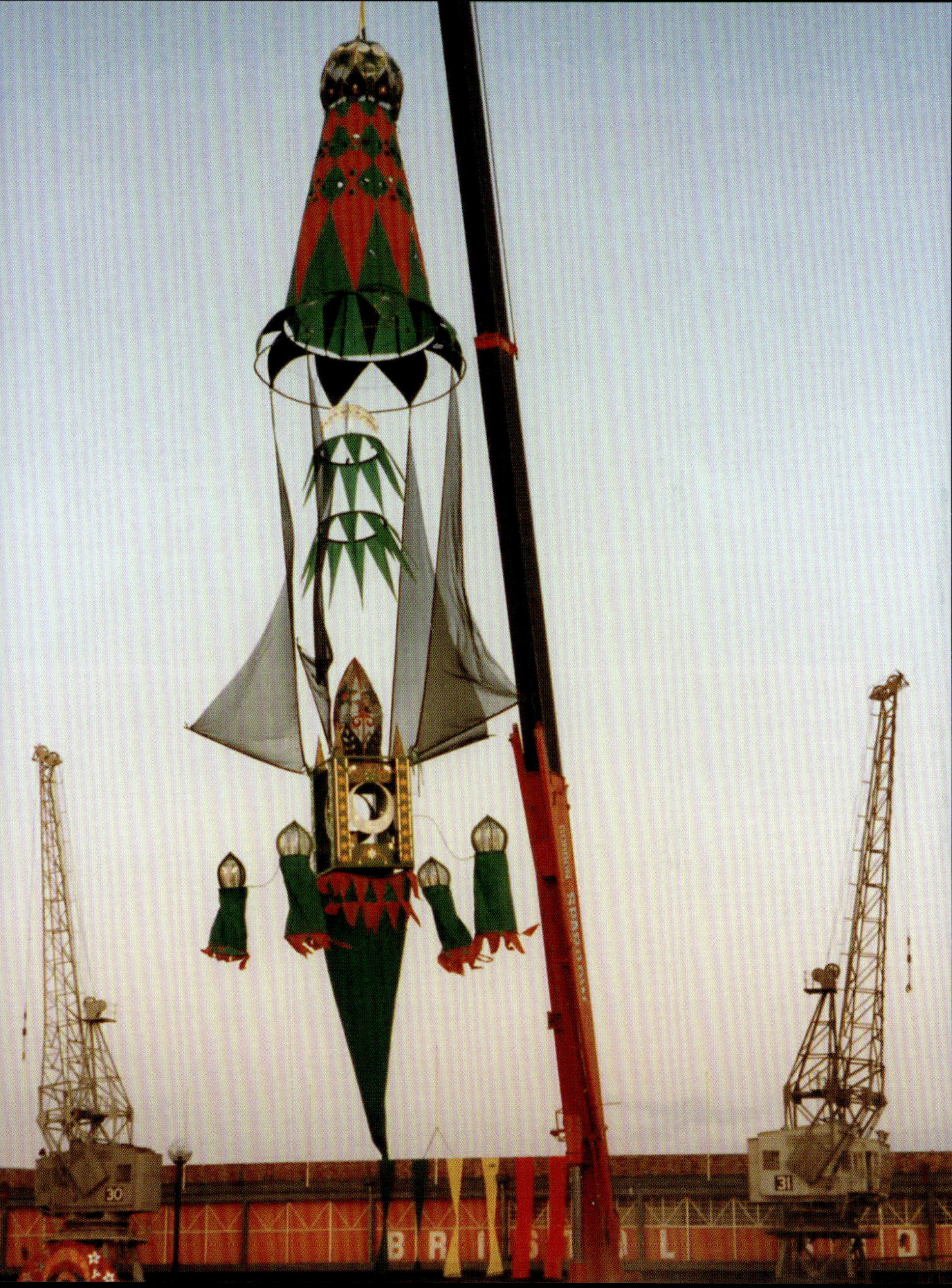

30
31
BRISTOL

Balraj Khanna 1940–2024
Apple Green 1991

Apple Green is part of a body of work that Balraj Khanna produced from the late 1970s onwards, in which ambiguous forms hover amid diffuse bounds of colour.[79] Here, as elsewhere, Khanna has modulated the field of colour with darker and lighter areas by using a tube or spray gun to blow paint across the surface, which he also covered in sand to build up texture. Using stencils, Khanna has introduced flamboyantly coloured, indeterminate forms (here, some resemble marine and avian creatures, while others recall paper boats, kites, hoops and other toys). Finally, the artist has used string to suggest the forms' plunging, twisting and darting trajectories. Critical discussions of this body of work seem to latently recognise its diasporic quality. Rasheed Araeen suggests that the forms' simultaneous proximity to childhood ephemera and to 'flotsam and jetsam' signifies 'an experience which is domestic as well as nomadic', while Kaushalia Khanna interprets the kinesis suggested by string as a 'journey . . . connecting the regions [Khanna] had come from and, perhaps, the new places he was going.'[80] We might draw out this recognition by reading Khanna's representation of drifting forms, his disconnection of the boundaries drawn by the canvas's edges from the forms' itineraries, and his dispersal of focal points across the painting, as amounting to a fundamentally diasporic reconstitution of pictorial space. This might be likened to Salman Rushdie's near-contemporaneous account of migration in the opening of *The Satanic Verses*, in which the protagonists are seen bursting out of an exploded aeroplane and hurtling through the sky: that 'most insecure and transitory of zones, illusory, discontinuous, metamorphic – because when you throw everything up in the air anything becomes possible'.[81]

Acrylic paint on canvas
114 x 114

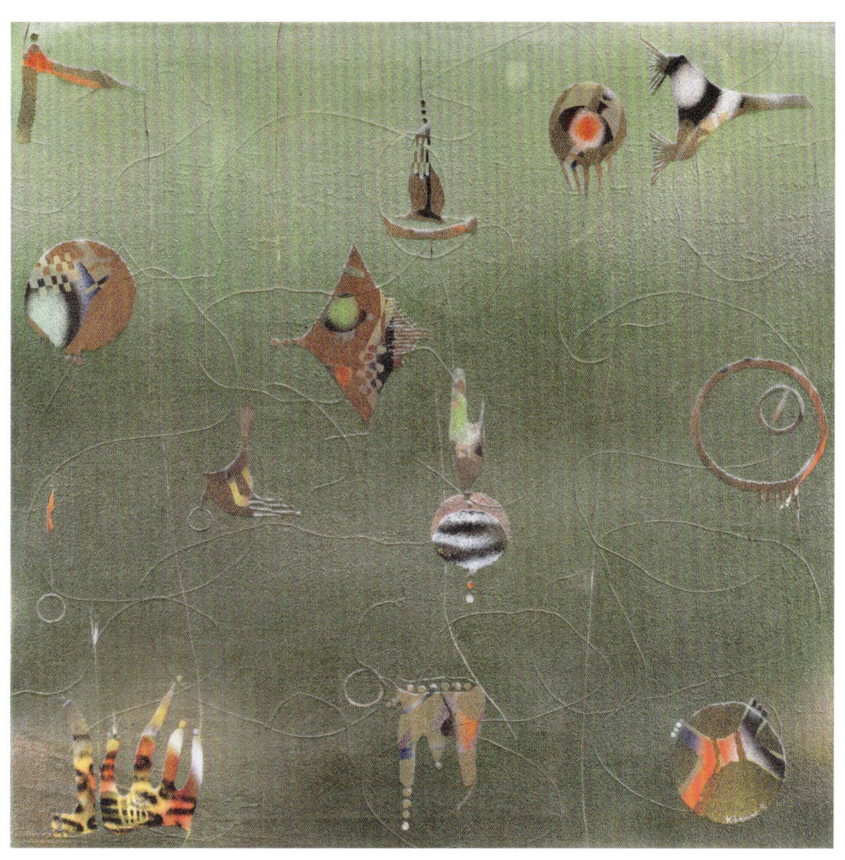

Alistair Raphael b.1966
Invasive Procedures 1991

Invasive Procedures was a photographic installation first exhibited at Alistair Raphael's solo exhibition at Camerawork, London in 1991. In this iteration, the work comprised three wall-based elements: two large, microscopic images of blood cells, one of which was pasted over a backlit Duratrans print of erupting sparks, and a photograph of a manhole cover pasted over an illuminated Duratrans print of another cell sample. The installation also included a floor-based element: an enlarged ultrasound scan superimposed over an architectural plan of the exhibition venue.[82] *Invasive Procedures* drew inspiration from Raphael's experience as a queer, diasporic subject during the AIDS epidemic. In resistance to moralising discourses about how queer bodies should behave, the work opened up a space for bodily exploration, where viewers could see how they felt in proximity to dramatically scaled-up images of the interior landscapes of other bodies, and when encountering backlit transparencies sealed over by epidermal photographs. Further, Raphael's pairing of medical imaging with representations of man-made systems made the viewer conscious of a possible analogy between biology and infrastructure, transforming the building itself into an opportunity for bodily enquiry. By plastering medical imaging across the gallery walls, Raphael equally intended to declare 'the institution as diseased', which may anticipate the philosopher Roberto Esposito's contention that the identification and management of contagion is essential to the maintenance of structures of domination.[83] Such had been exemplified by the moral panic of the 'gay plague', and by Margaret Thatcher's 1978 claim that anti-immigration legislation was required to stem the tide of immigrants threatening to 'swamp the nation'. In this context, *Invasive Procedures* transplants the metaphor of infection in public discourse from minority communities to institutions.

Detail comprising cyanotype, Duratrans C-type print and lightbox
100 x 100

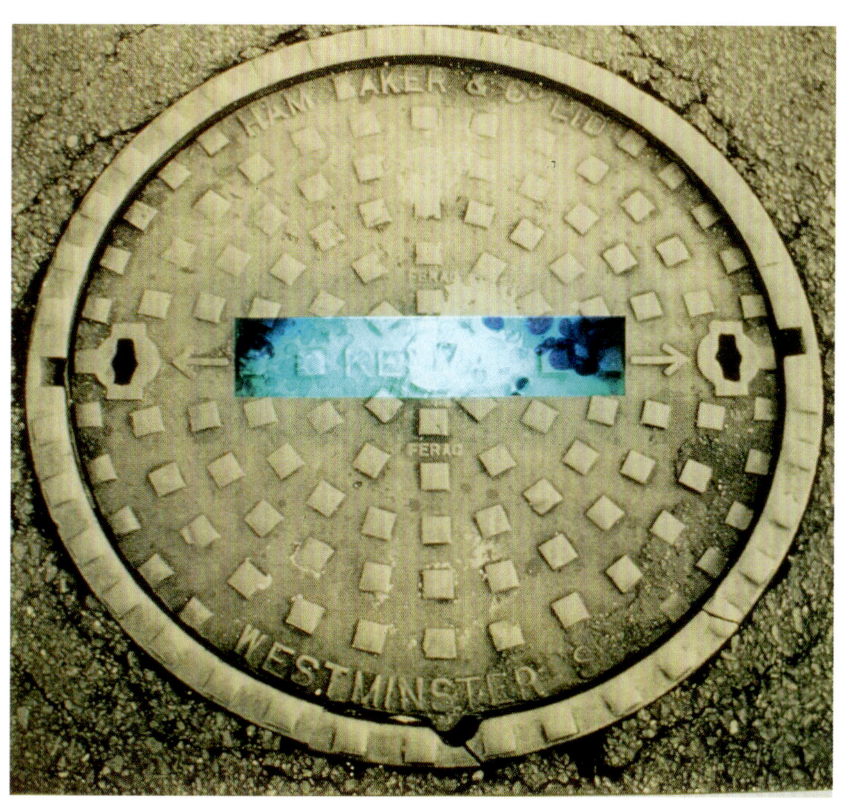
HAM BAKER & CO LTD
WESTMINSTER
PERAG

Veena Stephenson b.1962
Looking for Clues . . . Finding Them 1991

The installation *Looking for Clues . . . Finding Them* was exhibited at *A Table for Four*, an exhibition of four British South Asian feminist artists at the Bluecoat, Liverpool, in 1991. It comprised a series of 'clues' displayed on the gallery walls, alongside the text of the artwork's title. The 'clues' visible in this photograph include a drawing of a Kathakali mask – from the artist's parents' birthplace, Kerala – with its gaze cascading down a bolt of white fabric, which gathers into a pool on the gallery floor; in this pool of fabric is a Union Jack rendered in red conté pigment. A further 'clue' shown here is another drawing of a Kathakali mask, with torn edges. Born in Nairobi, Kenya, and raised in north-east London, Veena Stephenson was active in grassroots anti-racist and feminist cultural activism at the time of producing *Looking for Clues . . . Finding Them.* In this context, we can read the work's title as a reference to artist, and initiator of transcultural 'black' feminist artists' collectivism, Maud Sulter's oft-repeated statement that 'as Black women we read history for clues not facts', which she attributes to Black feminist writer Alice Walker (including in the 1990 anthology Sulter edited, *Passion: Discourses on Blackwomen's Creativity,* to which Stephenson contributed).[84] Along these lines, *Looking for Clues . . . Finding Them* resists the epistemological violence by which women of colour have been erased and distorted in dominant historical accounts and archival practices, by exploring the potential of the 'clue' to reconstitute history-making practices according to a transcultural 'black' feminist methodology. This is one that claims partialness rather than comprehensiveness, as well as favouring creative expression of women of colour over 'authentic' artefacts.

Detail comprising pastel, paper, sari and charcoal
400 x 100 and 100 x 100

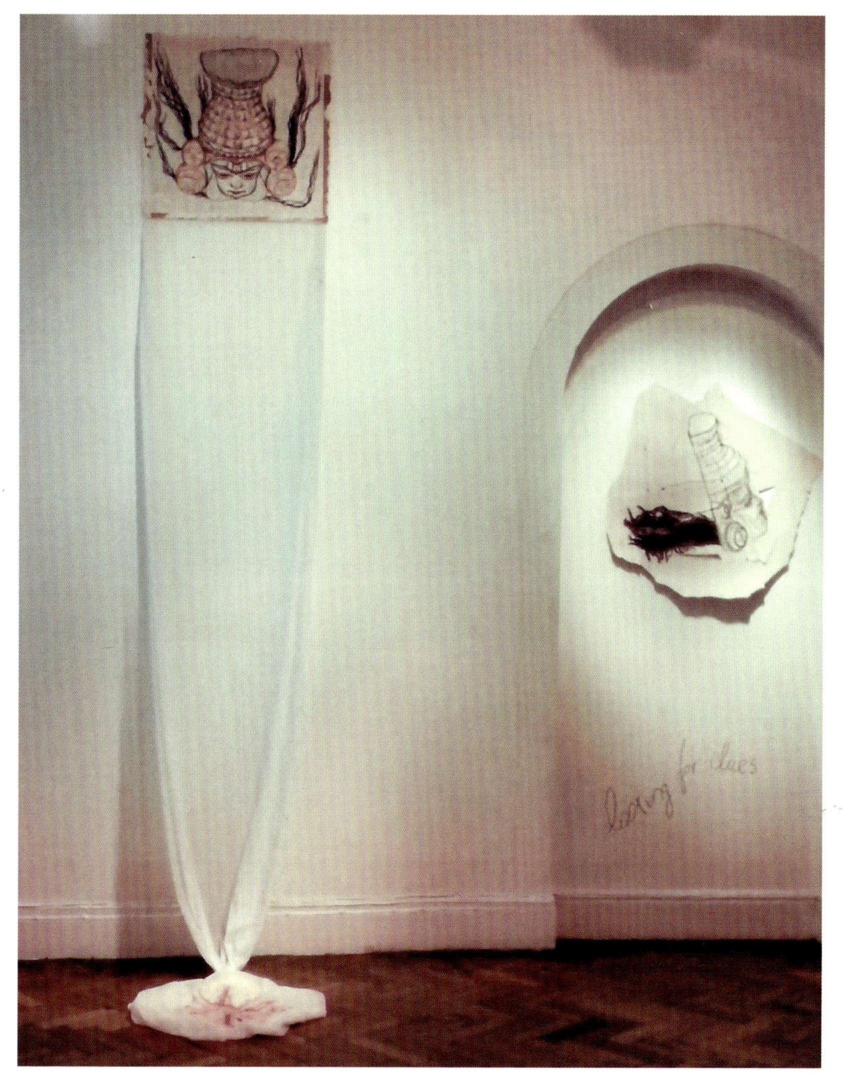
living for clues

Samena Rana 1955–92
(*Desk*) from the series *Bottom Drawer* 1991–2

Born in Lahore, Pakistan, Samena Rana relocated to Britain aged nine, to receive medical treatment following a car accident. Following her education, Rana travelled to Pakistan in 1982, where she developed an interest in photography. On returning, she enrolled in a photography course at the Sir John Cass School of Art, but was soon forced to quit due to the college's failure to facilitate wheelchair access. Instead, Rana developed her practice in the grassroots artistic movements of the 1980s, including community photography, feminism, the British Black Arts Movement and the Disability Arts Movement. This photograph of Rana at her desk exhibits elements of her distinctive photographic symbolism, as indexed in her poem published in *LINK* in 1991: her 'lost childhood', symbolised by 'bangles, black hair and the doll'; the rupture caused by the car accident, represented by the motif of the knife; the disruptive temporal effects of trauma, notably the irretrievability of the past, symbolised by clouds of 'blood and darkness' in her compositions; social 'barriers', notably ableism, racism and misogyny; and 'defiance', represented through the reclamation of symbols of her childhood, and of an objectifying gaze.[85] The photograph in question relates to the themes of defiance and reclamation: we see the artist reflected in a mirror on her desk, engrossed in the act of looking for herself. Meanwhile, Rana's desk is crowded with objects that form part of an oppositional self-fashioning – notably abundant make-up and jewellery, which can be read as reclaiming signifiers of South Asian femininity: adornment, sensuality and richness. Further, the presence of bangles – which evoke potent memories of sound and the play of light in Rana's poem – recuperate some of the sensations of her sundered childhood.

C-type photograph
Dimensions variable

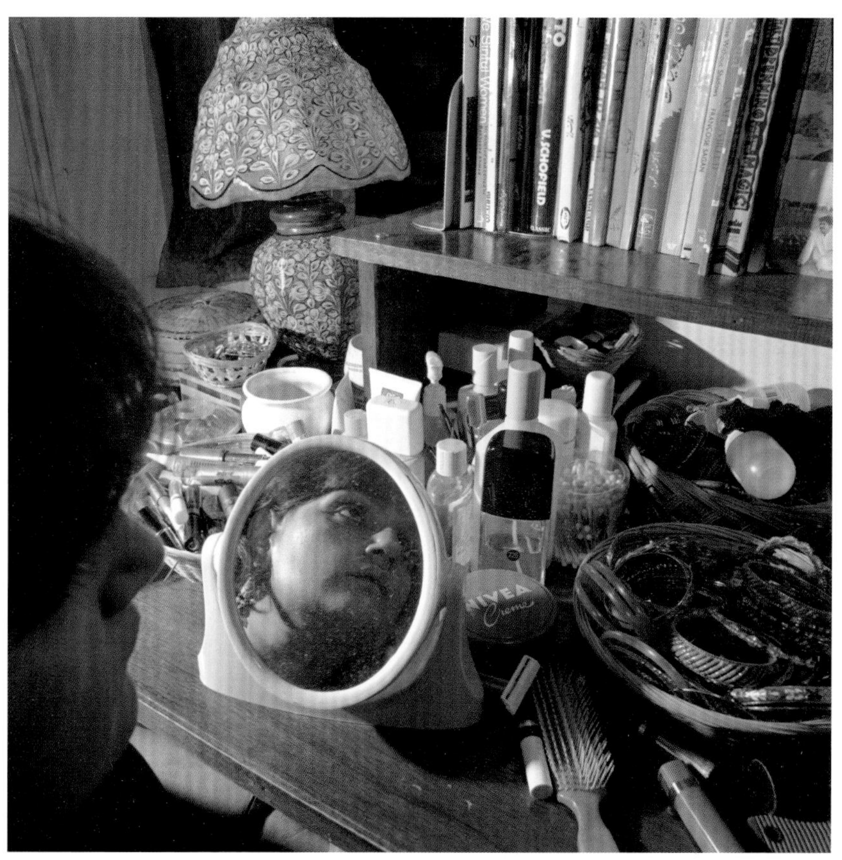

Fahmida Shah b.1966
Untitled 1992

Fahmida Shah's textile artwork makes distinctive use of expressive marks, loosely resembling architectural fragments, which are hand-painted onto silk. The material brings out the vibrancy and luminosity of the palette of fuchsia, yellow, purple and blue dyes, and gold and black inks. The prominence given to semi-spontaneous marks can be traced to Shah's training in textiles at Middlesex Polytechnic in the late 1980s, and particularly the teaching of Hugh McKinnon. McKinnon had trained as an artist before going into textiles, and had notably taken up his lecturer post in 1968: a year of global student agitation, including a sit-in at Hornsey College of Art (the forerunner of Middlesex Polytechnic) that entailed a wholesale rethinking of art education, the social role of art and the politics of design.[86] Shah recalls drawing influence from McKinnon's conception of textiles as a medium for creative expression, as opposed to a functional or commercial approach to the craft.[87] Also encouraged by McKinnon, Shah incorporated cultural influences from her upbringing in Pakistan and Kenya into her work; here, Shah adopts the brilliant palette of a Swahili kikoi, and of East, West and Central African kitenge.[88] Shah has explained her interest in textiles as deriving from the way in which, 'through textiles, the way you live can be wrapped around you. Through textiles, I can wrap myself and feel warm within that.'[89] In this light, by combining vitality, sensuousness and multicultural intertexts, the work in question can be interpreted as an experimental home for the diasporic subject. Further, the form of the sari, a garment wound repeatedly around the wearer (also seen in Sarbjit Natt's *Mughal*, p.139), accentuates the potential of any textile to constitute a bodily envelope.

Silk sari painted with silk dyes and inks
524 x 118

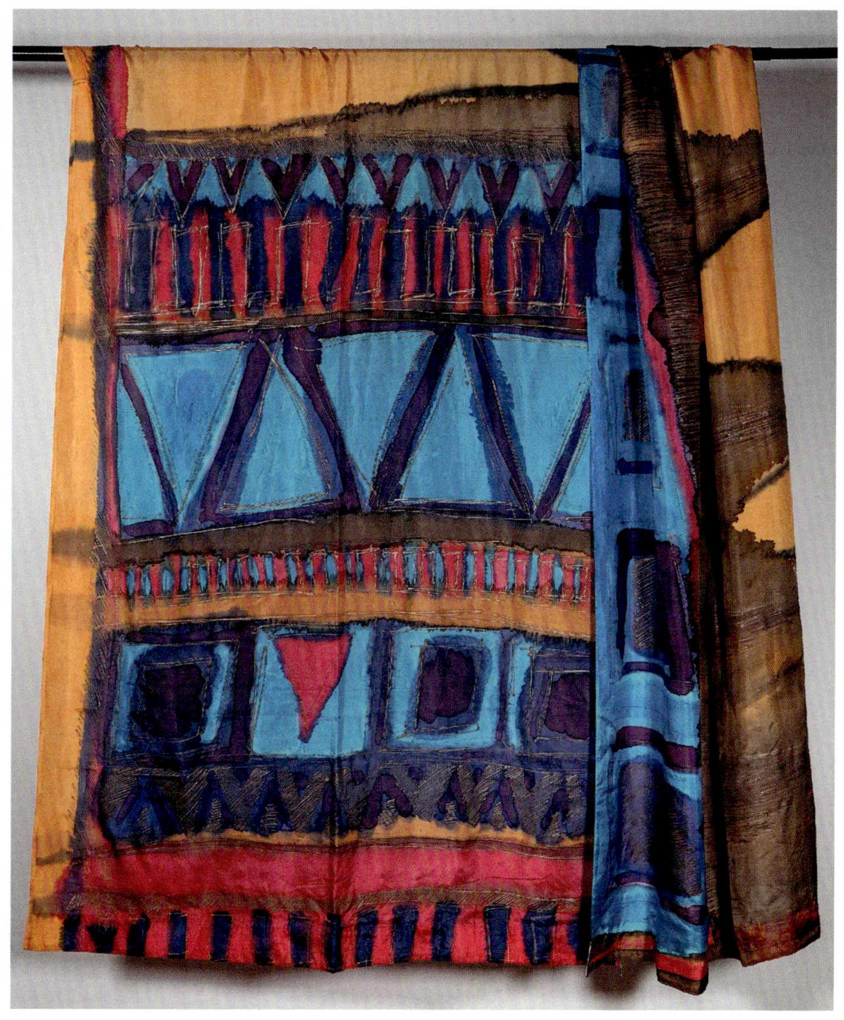

Gurminder Sikand 1960–2021
Enclosure 1992

Gurminder Sikand was born in Jamshedpur, India, in 1960, before growing up in the hill town of Kasauli, Himachal Pradesh. Sikand's family relocated to Britain in 1970, eventually settling in the Rhondda Valley in south Wales. She was based in Nottingham for the majority of her life, where she co-founded the Asian Artists' Group (AAG, meaning 'fire') with Said Adrus (see p.95) and Sardul Gill (see p.87). She was also involved in feminist contemporary art cultures, and the British Black Arts Movement. Her oeuvre began in the 1980s with works inspired by Madhubani devotional painting, in which figures in decorative settings are characterised by flat colouring and edge-to-edge patterning. By 1987 Sikand had begun working on paintings on large sheets of paper, crowded with figures, creatures and ornaments, and vividly rendered in gouache, often thickly applied; similar works were produced in pastel. Thirdly, in the 1990s, Sikand began producing smaller-scale works, combining transparent watercolour washes and opaque gouache, with a more neutral palette, and subtler line. These generally depict women and trees in landscape settings, and often cite early twentieth-century avant-garde representations of Arcadian subject matter and monumental women. *Enclosure* is from this period, representing the subject of Kali and Shiva, but with exclusively female figures. While Sikand was drawn to Kali as a representation of the tension between destruction and creation, the depiction of Kali pushing against a membrane also takes up her status as a symbol of resistance to social constraints facing women of colour – as explored in the work of Sutapa Biswas (p.59) and Nina Edge (p.73).

Gouache and ink on paper
29.4 x 20.8

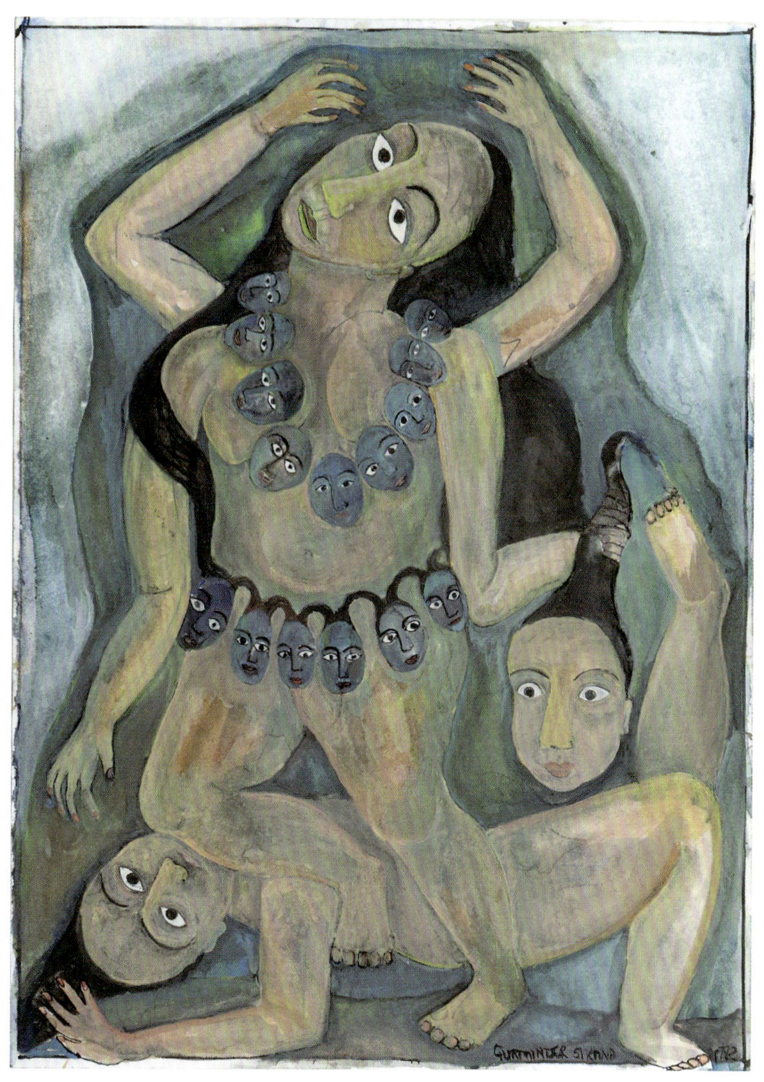

GURMINDER SIKAND

Gurinder Chadha b.1960
Bhaji on the Beach 1993

Bhaji on the Beach was the first full-length feature film by a British South Asian woman. It portrays an intergenerational group of South Asian women from Birmingham taking a day trip to Blackpool, including relaxing on the beach and enjoying bags of chips on the pier. Their leader is Simi, coordinator of Saheli Asian Women's Group, whose unapologetically hybrid identity (she wears a shalwar kameez and leather jacket) embodies the overall intention of the film: to refute binary representations of British South Asian femininity. While the film explores tensions between generations and identities, none of the characters are irredeemably Westernised or transmitters of a traditionalist culture. The character who is visiting from India is the most cosmopolitan, while the young, British-born characters have investments in tradition while also seeking to escape pressures from within their communities. As Gurinder Chadha has stated, 'There is a scale between each of these polarities' (South Asian or British, traditional or modern) 'and the film moves freely between them.'[90] This range and movement does not undermine the group's cohesion: the film ends with the women telling each other dirty jokes, signalling that community can coexist with social difference (not least through the sharing of laughter). Chadha's determination to represent British South Asian femininity on its own terms in *Bhaji on the Beach* can be seen as inheriting the politics of self-determination that has underpinned labour, anti-racist and feminist movements in Southall, west London – where Chadha grew up – since the early twentieth century.[91] At the same time, Chadha has actively sought to traverse grassroots and commercial cultural spheres: as she states, 'I make films that deal with my world through my eyes but funded by a "mainstream" sector.'[92]

35mm film
101 min

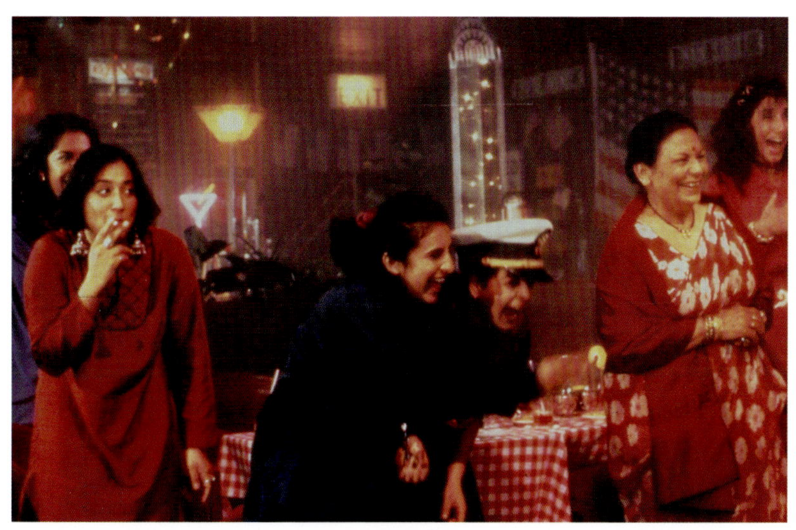

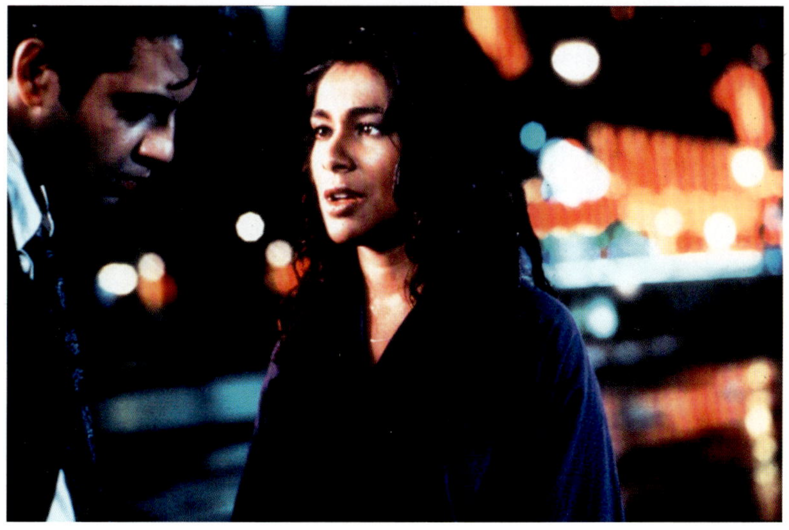

Bhajan Hunjan b.1956
Dialogue II 1993

Having arrived in Britain from Kenya to study fine art in 1975, Bhajan Hunjan
became involved in feminist activism in the early 1980s. This included
being a collective member of Reading's Asian women's refuge, Sahara, and,
in the context of scarcity of professional opportunities for British South
Asian women, co-curating the exhibition *Four Indian Women Artists* 1981–2
with Chila Kumari Singh Burman (see p.53) at the IAUK Gallery, London.
Dialogue II was made in the years after the artist's politicisation. It is a
large painting doubly divided in two: a figurative part on the left which
assumes the foreground, and a semi-abstract part on the right making up
the background. The foreground and background are divided by a pierced
screen, such as women would look out from in purdah. The figurative part
of the painting consists of portraits of two of the artist's nieces – one in
jeans and a T-shirt, the other in a saffron-coloured kameez – engaged in
conversation with each other. The abstract part of the work consists of a
luminescent orb, perhaps a sun or a moon; in its centre, burning through
the screen, is a fabric collage of floral embroidery made by the artist's
sister-in-law in Punjab. The title seems to refer to the multiple 'dialogues'
or exchanges that Hunjan sets up across the painting, including between
foreground and background; left and right; abstraction and figuration;
and, strikingly, between the South Asian and Western parts of South Asian
feminine cultural identity. We might consider the floral motif – which
pulsates between distinct realms of the painting – to be an indication of the
artist's feminist, diasporic ethics, one invested in the ongoing and open-
ended negotiation of difference.

Acrylic paint and fabric collage on canvas
156 x 214

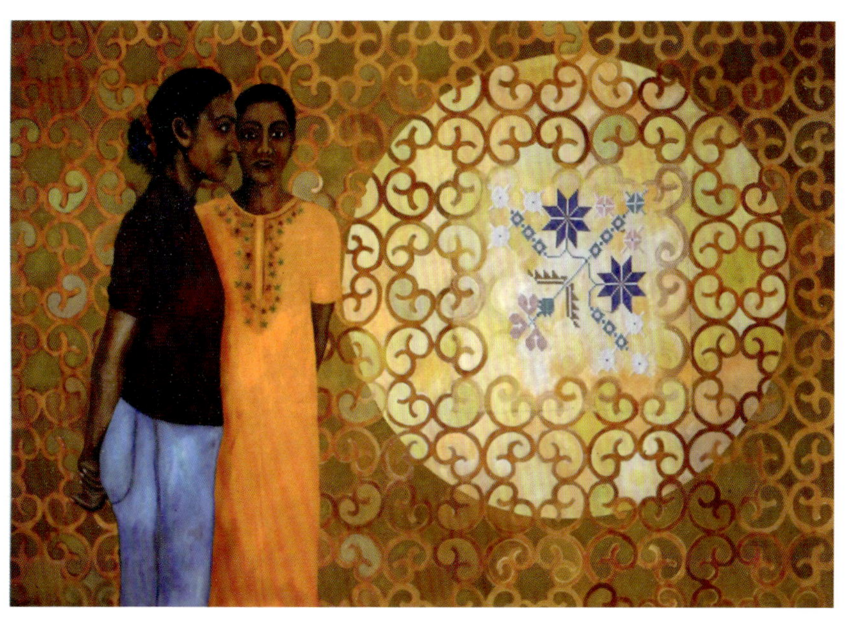

Permindar Kaur b.1965
Innocence 1993

Innocence was produced shortly after Permindar Kaur's relocation from Britain to Barcelona. There, the artist moved away from discourses based around identity – with which she had engaged as a participant in the British Black Arts Movement – and began working with fabric and colour. *Innocence* marks the pivot in Kaur's practice. It consists of various elements handmade by Kaur: a child's dress, which is dyed saffron – a sacred colour for Sikhs, including Kaur's family – bearing a kirpan, a sacred sword worn by Sikhs. These are set against a black background and within a box frame. In line with Kaur's oeuvre-defining straddling of dichotomies that relate, but are not reducible, to diasporic feminine subjectivity, *Innocence* elicits responses that oscillate between care and danger. The diminutive size of the dress urges the viewer to feel protective over this ghostly, petite figure, yet the knife thwarts this with the threat of fatal harm – a paradox reinforced by the work's contrasting materials of cotton and iron. As with many of Kaur's works – such as gargantuan cots and teddy bears with devil horns – the overall effect is one of deep unease. However, this feeling may be understood as a truthful response to the ambivalence of the diasporic feminine experience: one that resists the urge to resolve it either way – to be impaled on the horn of such categories as 'domestic' or 'public' – and which instead commits to it. As Kaur herself summarises her artistic and critical approach: 'I always wanted my work to be at a point of balance where you didn't know which side the work fell on.'[93]

Cotton and iron

60 x 72

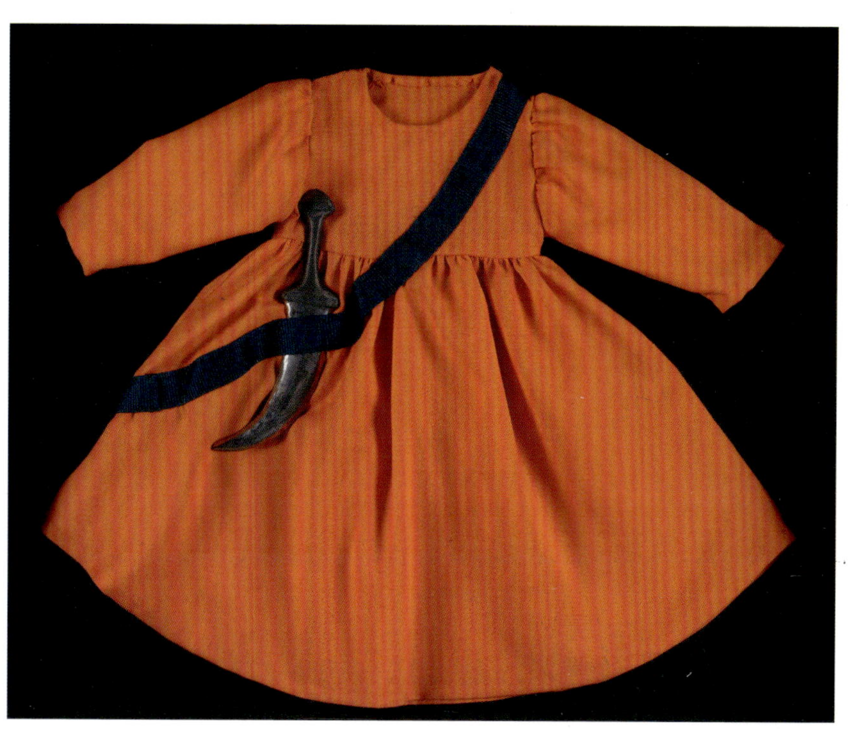

Nilofar Akmut b.1956
Dear Women of the Indian Subcontinent 1994

Dear Women of the Indian Subcontinent (*DWOTIS*) forms part of a body
of work in which Nilofar Akmut applied a feminist artistic methodology to
the histories of partition and independence. This photograph shows the
work's installation at the 4th Asian Art Show, Fukuoka, in 1994. It comprises
a set of lightboxes arranged in a linear, asymmetrical formation around three
perpendicular gallery walls. One of the lightboxes displays an image of an
upside-down map of the South Asian subcontinent, over which the artist
has drawn a pair of spreadeagled legs. The remaining images are of natural
elements (fire, the sea and a leaf fossil); synthetic objects (syringes, hanging
balls and horseshoes); and an abstract artwork, each of which serves as a
symbol of a specific anti-colonial activist who was a woman.[94] In the centre
of the installation is a vitrine encasing incinerated photos of the activists,
entangled in wire and lit from beneath by a single lightbulb. In *DWOTIS*, Akmut
carries forward elements of previous works in her series on partition and
independence, including the recovery of women's contributions to liberation
struggles, and the motif of the upside-down embellished map.[95] The work
continues her examination of the use of women to project and sublimate
feelings of hope, desire and fear (such as the metaphor of the 'birth' of new
nations), while insisting on the realities of women's pain (especially evoking the
trauma of rape that approximately 100,000 women endured during partition)
as well as their strength and political agency.[96] At the same time, *DWOTIS*
sees Akmut explore new degrees of poeticism and abstraction, while also
deepening the complexity of her historiographical approach: here, images of
violence, immolation, penetration and collective struggles for freedom vibrate
together as incommensurable parts of the history of decolonisation.

Lightboxes, vitrine, lightbulb, wire, paper and photographic negatives
400 x 500 x 600

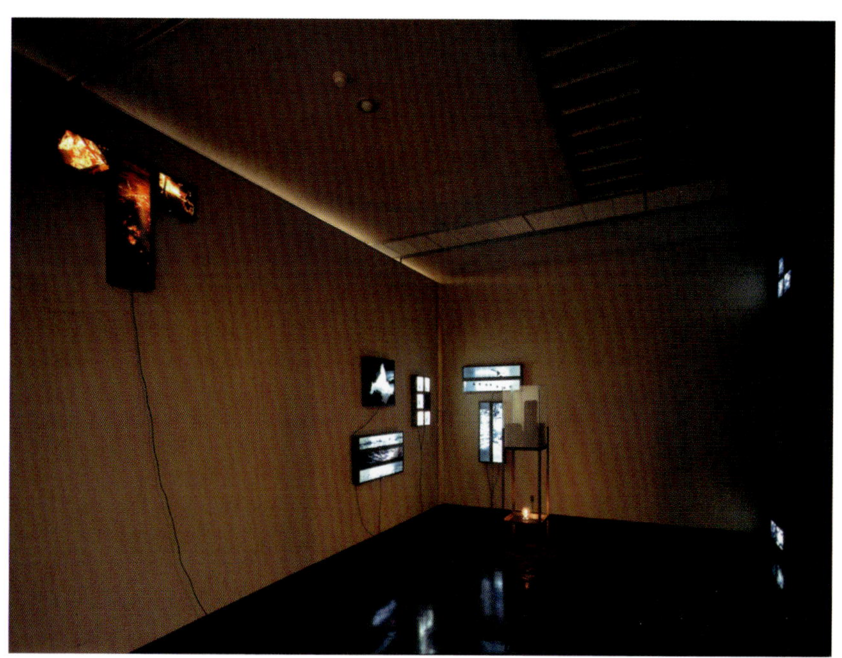

Juginder Lamba b.1948
Lovers 1994

Since the age of seventeen, Juginder Lamba has been drawn to the myth of Icarus, which, for him, 'encapsulates . . . our impulses to soar above the material conditions and narrow explanatory historicism that assigns each to his/her proper place . . . and to seek to incorporate those impulses into new strategies for survival and new expressions of hope'.[97] The 'assignment' of people to their 'proper place' insinuates the colonial and postcolonial identity categories with which the artist has long been concerned. This includes the consolidation of 'Hindu' and 'Muslim' identities upon the partition of India, which forced his non-Muslim parents to leave their home in the north-west of Punjab when it became part of West Pakistan; the racial categories that segregated the Kenyan society into which he was born in a position of relative privilege; the categories of 'immigrant . . . alien . . . outsider' that he was assigned when he moved to England in 1962;[98] and, finally, the progressive, identity-based movements of the 1970s to 1990s, in which he was a critical participant. *Lovers* is a testament to the inspiration Lamba draws from the myth of Icarus for producing common values through cultural difference. It comprises a wooden sculpture of two figures embracing beneath a shelter. It layers references to Lamba's plural cultural heritage, including the temple sculptures he has cited as having found inspirational during his time in India, and Makonde sculpture.[99] Consistent with the artist's social vision, these are conduits for a meditation on a transcendental theme.

Wood
27 x 88 x 45

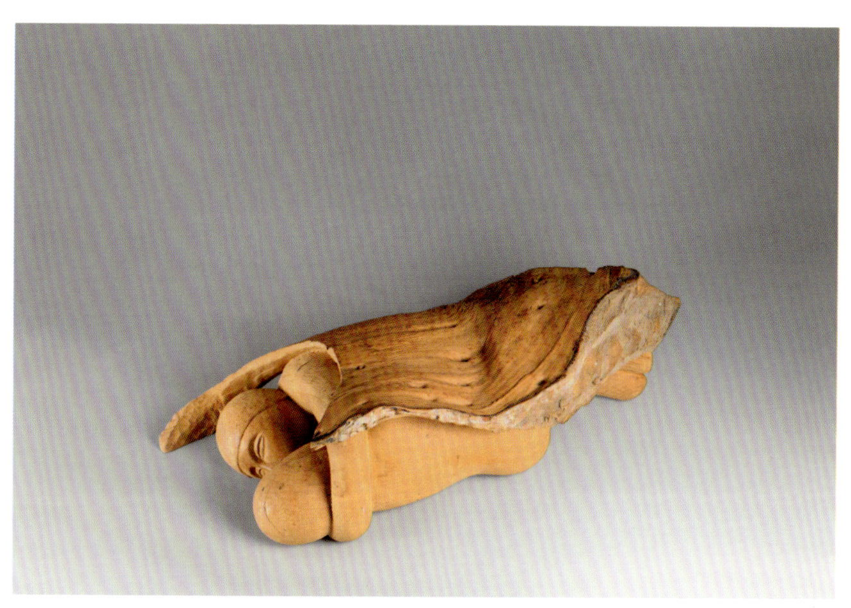

Anita J. McKenzie b.1958
Mother and Daughter from the series *Imaging the Black Family* 1994

Following her activity in feminist and anti-racist photography circles in the 1980s, Anita J. McKenzie produced *Imaging the Black Family*: a series of black-and-white portraits of families of colour. The series addresses the politicised subject of the diasporic family in Britain: pathologised by the state as unstable, as in the case of African Caribbean families, or as traditionalist, as in the case of South Asian families; at the same time, both an important source of safety and affirmation away from a racially structured public sphere, and site of intergenerational transmission of tactics and strategies for resisting racism; and finally, a pressured formation by communities of colour themselves, such as the injunction to reproduce caste and patriarchy within South Asian families. McKenzie's photographs reflect this complex historical reality, challenging conventional expectations that 'the black family' is only one thing; that family is a black-and-white affair. McKenzie depicts a variety of sitters, from triplets to mixed-heritage families, and fathers and sons. *Imaging the Black Family* was devised as a public education resource, comprising eighteen framed prints that could be hired by community centres, schools and libraries. One of its exhibition venues was the Stephen Lawrence Gallery, University of Greenwich (2003), which extended the series's engagement with the family as a site of anti-racist struggle. The gallery was founded in 2000 by Paul Stigant in close partnership with Doreen Lawrence, who had been a student at the University in 1993 when her son, Stephen Lawrence, a talented artist and designer, and supporter of artists in his community, was murdered in a racist attack. As writer and academic Jacqueline Rose has argued, Doreen Lawrence's activism has challenged the depoliticisation of grieving mothers, whereby 'a mother can suffer, she can be the object of heartfelt empathy', but she must never '[tell] the world of the political and social ills behind the death of a child'.[100]

Ilford film
60.9 x 60.9

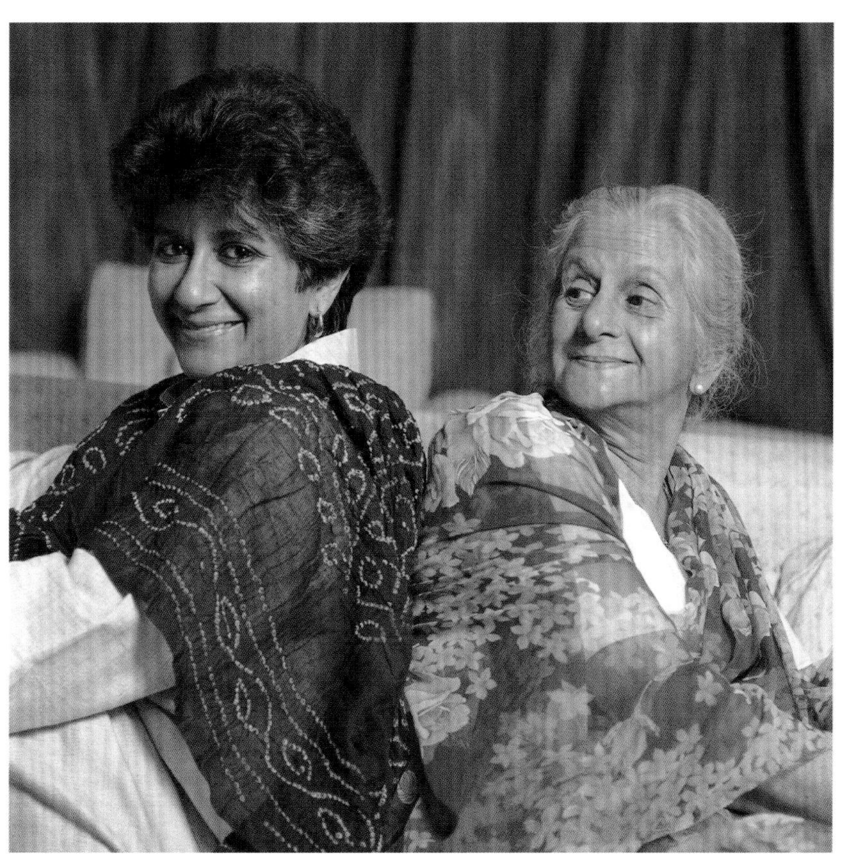

Fatima Ahmed b.1934
Untitled 1995

This painting is a culmination of Fatima Ahmed's lifelong and career-spanning concern with the politics of gender, and might be thought of as a continued reflection on questions raised in the international modernist contexts in which Ahmed experienced her artistic formation. The painting comprises a strikingly vertical canvas, divided into two unequal parts: an upper section depicting a tree in concentric square frames, and a lower section depicting a woman in concentric rectangular frames. The palette is at once vibrant and restrained – shocking pink simply modulated with white – while the figurative elements are rendered as subtle and hazy. By depicting a female figure claiming an autonomous space, and, through its opacity, withholding part of her appearance from the viewer's gaze and reserving it for the figure herself, the work registers the artist's attentiveness to gender injustice. This spanned her exposure to the Women's Liberation Movement in 1970s London, having relocated from Bombay, and then to the Indian Women's Movement on her return to India shortly thereafter. Further, the work has roots in questions around Indian modernity circulating when Ahmed trained as an artist at the College of Fine Arts in Hyderabad in the late 1950s, and which still held interest in the group exhibitions in which she participated in London (including *Five Indian Artists* with Jatin Das, Lancelot Ribeiro (see p.33), Mohan Sharma and F.N. Souza (see p.27) at Arts 38 in 1976). This painting seems to illustrate a feminist vision of Indian modernity: both a tree – a key symbol of 'Indianness', as elaborated in discussion of Prem Lata Chandra's work (p.23) – and a woman are shown in simultaneous emergence.

Oil paint on canvas
109.2 x 54.6

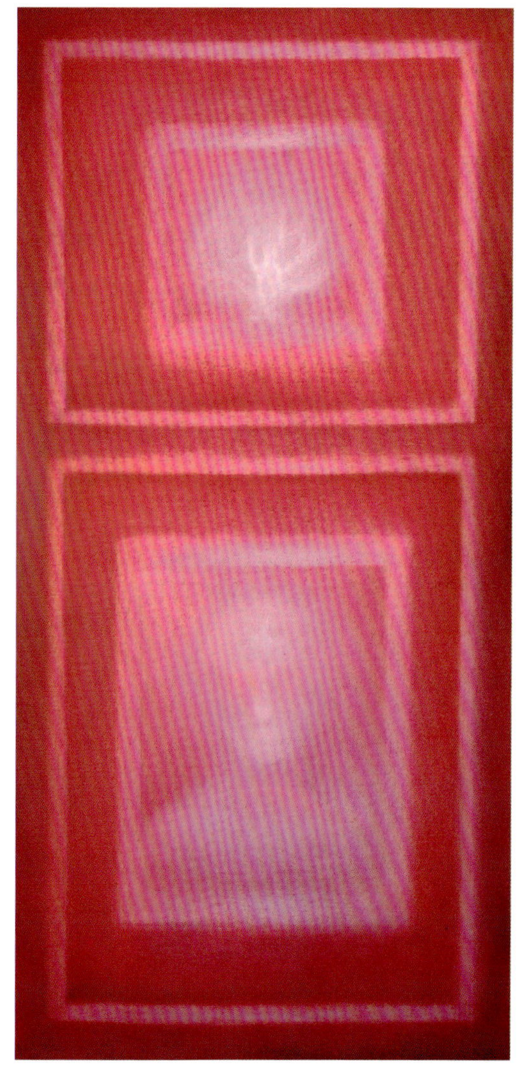

Jai Chuhan b.1955
Self Portrait 1995

In her words, Jai Chuhan conceives of each of her paintings as 'a fluctuating
psychological space [in which] a sense of movement, rhythm and flow,
improvised around a basic idea, is conveyed'.[101] The 'basic idea' in *Self Portrait*
is the reconsideration of artistic subjectivity in the light of motherhood and
migration. In the centre of an interior space, we see the artist dishevelled,
crouched down, holding a paintbrush in her hand beside a pile of paint-
daubed rags; the use of impasto, thick brushstrokes, and raw, fleshy colours
to depict her body starkly conveys the material effects of working to sustain
an artistic practice during early motherhood. Indeed, this painting can be
situated in the context of a broader tendency concerned with the realities of
being an artist and a mother simultaneously (finding expression in the 1993
exhibition *Reclaiming the Madonna: Artists as Mothers* that toured around
England and Wales, in which Chuhan was included).[102] In the background of
the painting, emerging from a bathroom, is a portrait of Chuhan when she
was pregnant, rendered in delicate brushstrokes and pastel colours that
convey the artist's love for the memory of her pregnancy. Meanwhile, on a
rear wall is a rendering of an ancient Indian temple sculpture copied from a
book in the artist's studio. Beneath, Chuhan's child emulates the tribhanga
pose of a sculpture. Altogether, *Self Portrait* might be read as a lucid enquiry
into artistic practice in the contexts of motherhood and diaspora, as well
as a commitment to it. The work highlights the labour of artmaking and
motherhood, while also sustaining an investment in art as a space in which it
might be possible to cohere the layered temporalities of both diaspora and
motherhood.

Oil paint on canvas
210 x 150

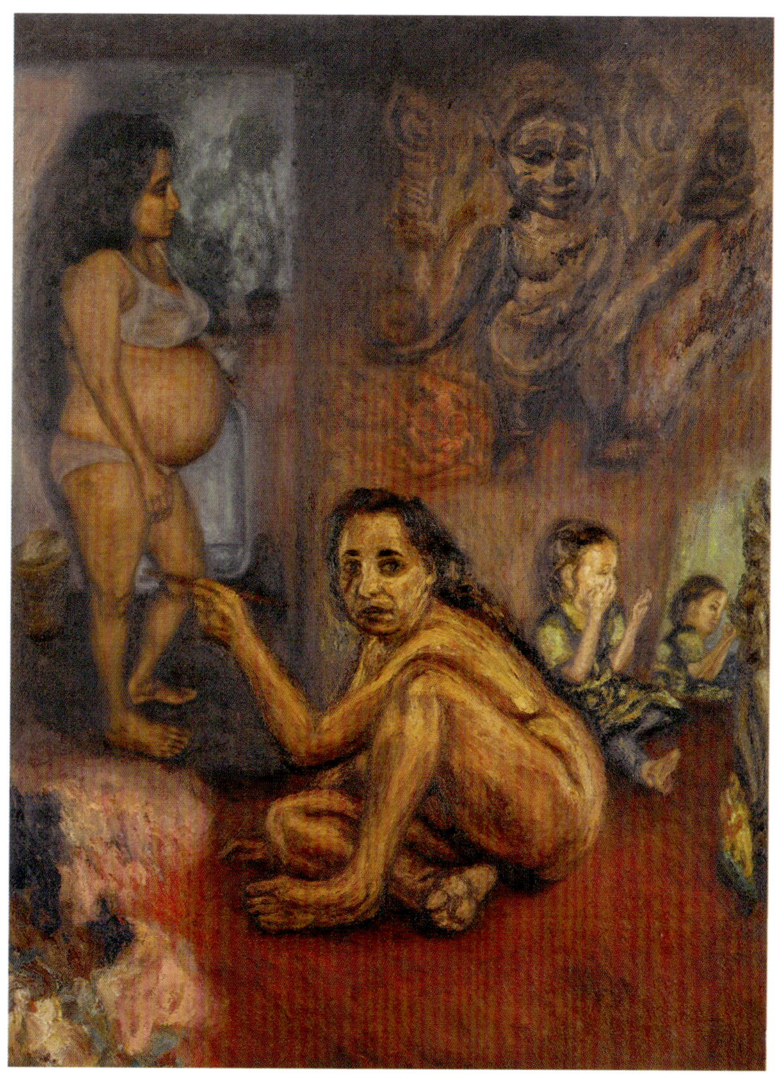

Sarbjit Natt b.1962
Mughal 1996

Mughal is a textile artwork evoking forms of socio-religious pluralism. It is a silk sari – a garment worn by the women in Sarbjit Natt's family – painted with jewel-coloured Mughal architectural motifs arranged in orderly rows, with a band of 'sky' streaked with pale yellow and jade green. The work deploys Natt's experimental technique of beginning with freehand drawing on the fabric, before applying gutta (a rubber-based metallic outline) and then painting on colour. Two years before completing *Mughal*, Natt wrote of her concern for historical and contemporary nationalisms, including the partition of India, which her parents witnessed first-hand in her birthplace, Ludhiana; the Rushdie Affair;[103] and an ascendant Hindu nationalism in India. She concluded with the question, 'Can we all gain strength from cooperation, or is separation the way forward?'[104] *Mughal* explores the possibility of renewing a pluralist social fabric by combining motifs drawn from Mughal architecture (perhaps a gesture of tribute to the Babri Masjid, which was destroyed by Hindu nationalists in 1992) with multiculturalist material culture: the artist incorporates the structured and formal layouts of phulkari and bagh embroidery, which, according to her research, relied on collaborations between Muslim cotton-weavers and Hindu and Sikh embroiderers, in pre-partition Punjab. Natt's artwork especially emphasises women's production of multiculturalist social relations: she was drawn to phulkari and bagh as textiles made by women.

Tissue silk with gutta outlines infilled with paint
168.5 x 110

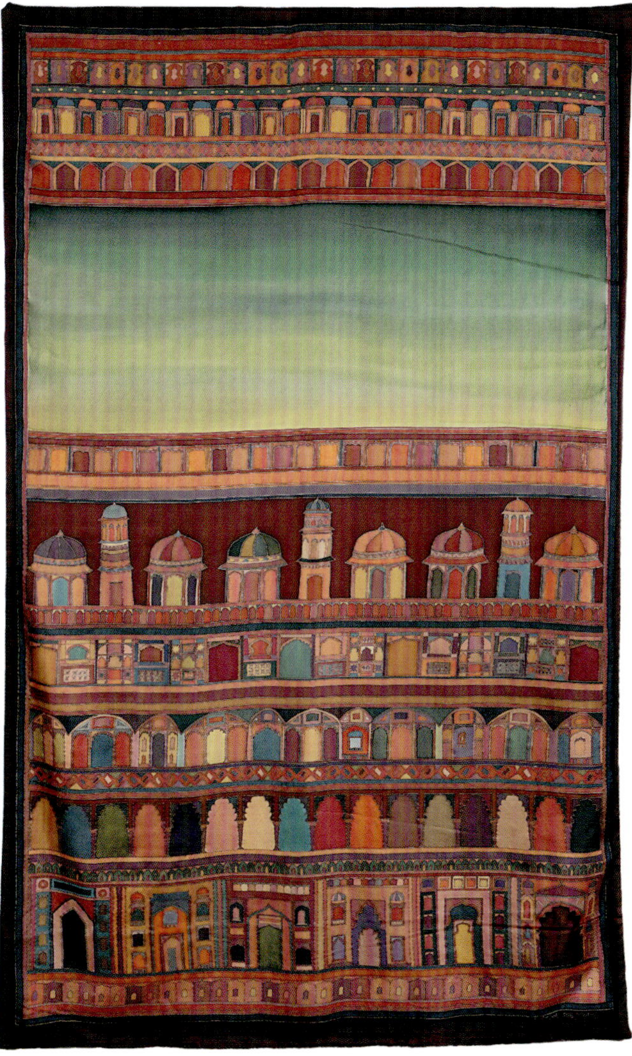

Mohini Chandra b.1964
album pacifica 1997

The installation *album pacifica* might be described as a micro-history of the
Indo-Fijian diaspora, to which the artist and her family belong.[105] The work
shares family photographs gathered from Mohini Chandra's relatives, but
only the back of them, so that the viewer is forced to draw conclusions from
the immediate material contexts of the photographs. These include clues as
to their use (for instance, residues of Sellotape, creases or teacup rings); a
sense of their age depending on their level of degradation; and snippets of
information offered in handwritten annotations. In the book version of the
artwork (2001), the sequence of photographs builds a narrative, communicated
to the artist by her relatives via their captions: 'Mohini, This your aunt Puspa
who now lives in Auckland N.Z.'. While unfolding this family history, Chandra
inserts touches of humour: one group portrait bears the caption 'NICE . . . NICE
. . . UGLY'. There are also poignant moments: a caption shown here reads 'Died
in New Zealand on 13 October 1971', giving the reader information about the
photographic subject's death, but denying the representation of their life on the
front side of the print. By disclosing the intimacies inscribed on the reverse of
photographs, yet withholding the images themselves, Chandra offers viewers
a close engagement with lived histories of postcolonial migration, conveying
an especially powerful impression of the pain of migration and the tightness
of kinship bonds. The gesture also speaks back to the history of colonial
photography, especially Western photographers' expectation of the visual
availability of colonised people, and the privilege afforded to them of seeing
all from behind the camera. Even if such photographs, on close inspection,
routinely contested this binary schema, it remains striking that Chandra extends
her subjects a protection denied by historical photographic cultures.

Photographs, fibre, wax and toner
100 parts each 20 x 25

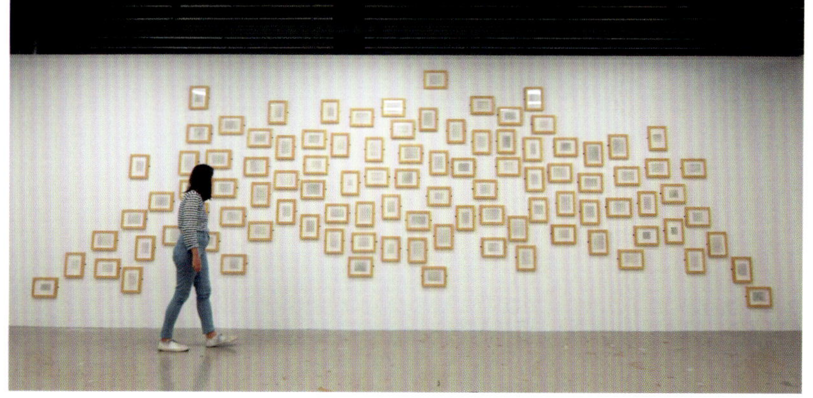

Ian Iqbal Rashid b.1968
Surviving Sabu 1997

Surviving Sabu is a film about the making of a film: Amin, a second-generation, gay British South Asian, enlists his reluctant father, Sadru, to appear in a film relating racism in contemporary Britain to the career of Indian-born Hollywood actor Sabu, who starred in films including *The Thief of Baghdad* 1940. Ian Iqbal Rashid interweaves takes from Amin's film with scenes of clashes between Amin and Sadru at home, arising from their opposing reactions to the injunctions of race, gender and sexuality. Sadru has model minority aspirations, and disapproves of Amin's sexuality, while Amin is deeply committed to anti-racist and LGBTQ+ social movements. This polarity is articulated through their responses to Sabu: Sadru finds in him a source of post-racial hope, while Amin claims he is 'a colonialist fantasy'. Yet, Rashid posits that cinema (encompassing both filmmaking and fandom) is a site for the transformation of interpersonal relationships. As father and son collaborate on Amin's film, and re-watch their favourite films starring Sabu on the sofa together, they begin to negotiate their antagonism. In an aside, Amin reflects that his father's choice to rebuild his life in diaspora 'so his son could have a better life' was courageous. Meanwhile, as queer theorist Gayatri Gopinath observes, a scene in which father and son indulge in the intimacy of sharing a cigarette, and gaze at Sabu's body together, shows both characters participating in an experience of queer desire 'that is produced through and against dominant culture.'[106] In sum, *Surviving Sabu* can be understood as an exploration of the socially reconstitutive potential of cinema, especially in the context of queer diaspora.

16mm film
16 min

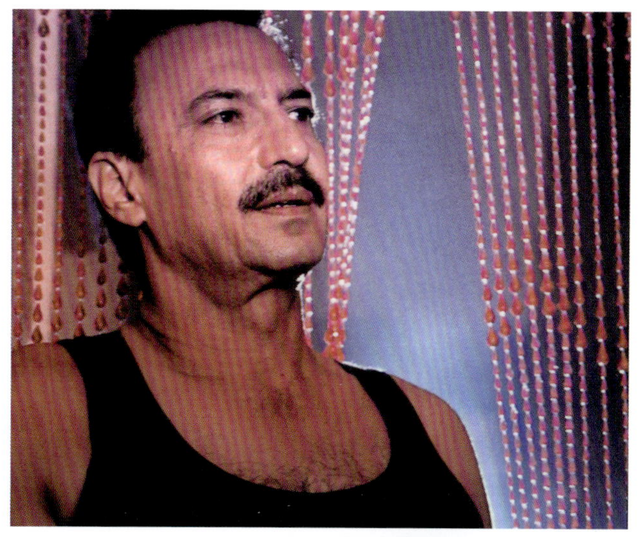

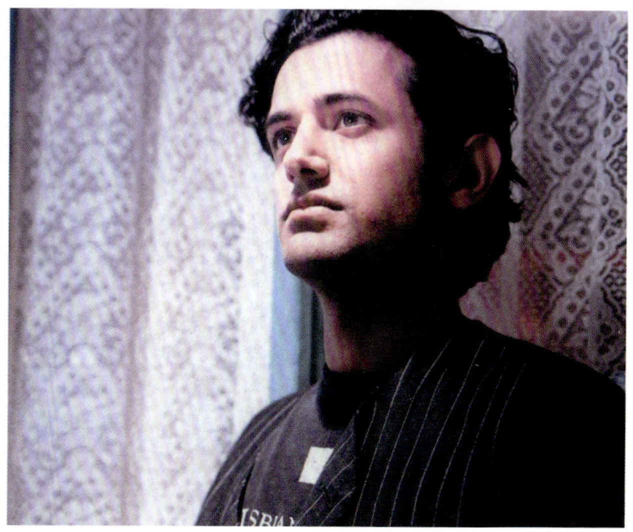

Ali Mehdi Zaidi b.1963
Of Fears and Desires 1997

Of Fears and Desires is a sculpture consisting of an aluminium column
with Perspex panels through which the spectator views a backlit image of
a young hand tenderly cupping a pair of older hands, infinitely reflected in
a double mirror. Ali Mehdi Zaidi made the work shortly before his father's
passing in Lahore, the city Zaidi had left in 1988 to further his artistic
training in London. In the first instance, this work is about stemming loss:
the use of the infinity mirror allows Zaidi's photograph of tender contact
to recur in a never-ending succession, exemplifying film theorist Emma
Wilson's notion that art can offer a mourner 'a form of pain management,
. . . a means, through creativity, . . . of bringing some moderation, relief
or pursued contact' with a deceased loved one.[107] At the same time, the
work offers a subversive account of a father-son relationship: the hands in
the photograph are not those of Zaidi and his father, but of Zaidi and the
father of Keith Khan (p.109), Zaidi's life partner and artistic collaborator
at the time, with whom he ran the collective Motiroti from 1996. As Zaidi
recollects, Khan's father was a 'surrogate father' to him in London.[108] In this
sense, *Of Fears and Desires* represents the mediation of Zaidi's grief over
the impending loss of his father through additional paternal relationships
formed through queer and diasporic kinship. As such, the work entails
a transformation of the conventional father-son relationship, in which
paternal bonds can be multiplied and distributed along other vectors of
connection.

Perspex, mirror, aluminium and Duratrans
94 x 30.5 x 30.5

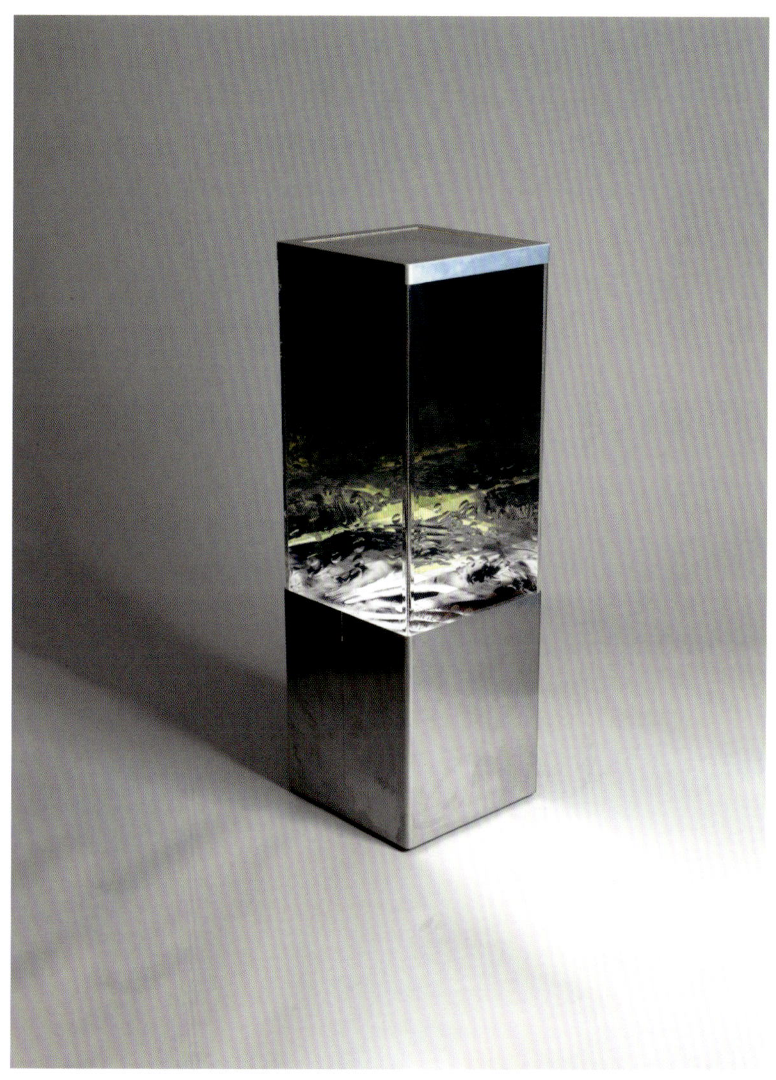

Saleem Arif Quadri b.1949
Landscape of Longing 1997–9

In 1982, Saleem Arif Quadri began experimenting with cut-outs partly
inspired by Matisse's gouaches découpées, which he developed over
time into block-board cut-outs mounted on wooden supports, floating
freely off the wall. Once installed, negative spaces within and between
the cut-outs form recognisable symbols. Quadri describes this practice
as having invented a 'volumetric space': 'a third dimension to my pictorial
language'.[109] *Landscape of Longing* is a striking example of this method. The
work is made up of seven three-dimensional cut-outs that each comprise
a distinctive, free-floating form, while also coming together to achieve a
unitary composition. Each of the cut-outs has a densely textured, expressive
surface: the artist used oil paint on acrylic mixed with sand, and raking
gestures, so that the forms resemble ploughed fields seen from above. In
the first instance, *Landscape of Longing* might be interpreted – in a manner
that recalls the work of Balraj Khanna (p.111) – as manifesting a migratory
conception of space: one whereby incongruous parts can somehow
fit together, just as the distinction between the 'inside' and 'outside' of
the artwork has been overhauled. An additional reading might be drawn
from the work's jubilant mood, transmitted via its sense of free-spirited
movement; its use of colour (mostly brilliant blues and greens worked into
the furrows of its impasto surfaces); and its symbolism (a flower in the
far-left cut-out conveys a burst of new life, while an oil lamp in the far-right
cut-out symbolises a progression from darkness into light). This sense of
positive transformation might be related to developments in the artist's life
at the time: meeting his wife, and securing a studio in London, which, as he
recalls, brought fulfilment after years of instability.[110]

---

7 works on wood, muslin, acrylic paint and oil paint
Overall display 210 x 420 x 6.5

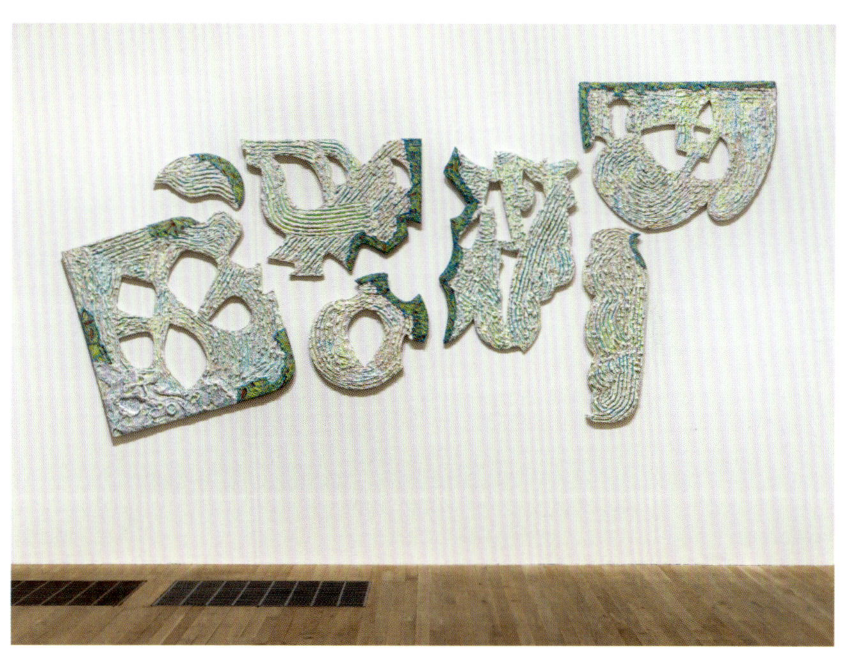

Parminder Sekhon b.1968
Wedding Guests of the Bride 2002

This photograph is one of Parminder Sekhon's staged portraits of her fellow participants in London's South Asian queer scene. It depicts two figures in front of a poster for the film *Devdas* 2002. The figure on the right adopts the pose of a Hindi cinema hero, eyes smouldering and jacket slung irreverently over one shoulder, or perhaps of a model. Meanwhile, the figure on the left, wearing a resplendent garland, grins cheerily at the camera. The sitters are situated within an elaborate web of desiring gazes, as the actresses in the poster (Aishwarya Rai and Madhuri Dixit) look out seductively, while, comically, the hero (Shah Rukh Khan), looks downwards in anguish and lust at Sekhon's right-hand sitter. If poet and novelist Cherry Smyth has written that Sekhon makes work that contests the enforced invisibility of queer South Asian subjects by '[manoeuvring] into the gaps' of visual culture, then where this work 'manoeuvres' is into Hindi films, fashion magazines and commercial advertising.[111] South Asian queerness had been, and to a large extent continues to be, absent from these crucial sites for the formation of queer South Asian identities, despite the increase in white queer representation at the turn of the 2000s. More implicitly, the work is also a document of the consolidation of a queer South Asian community at the time; so much is suggested by the protective gesture of the sitters placing their arms around each other's shoulders. The photograph's generosity of rich, warm reds and golds invites the viewer to be enfolded into this collective; as Smyth writes, 'highly glossy, sexy and vibrant with lush colour – if you weren't gay or lesbian, these [works] would make you reconsider'.[112]

Fuji colour reversal film
Dimensions variable

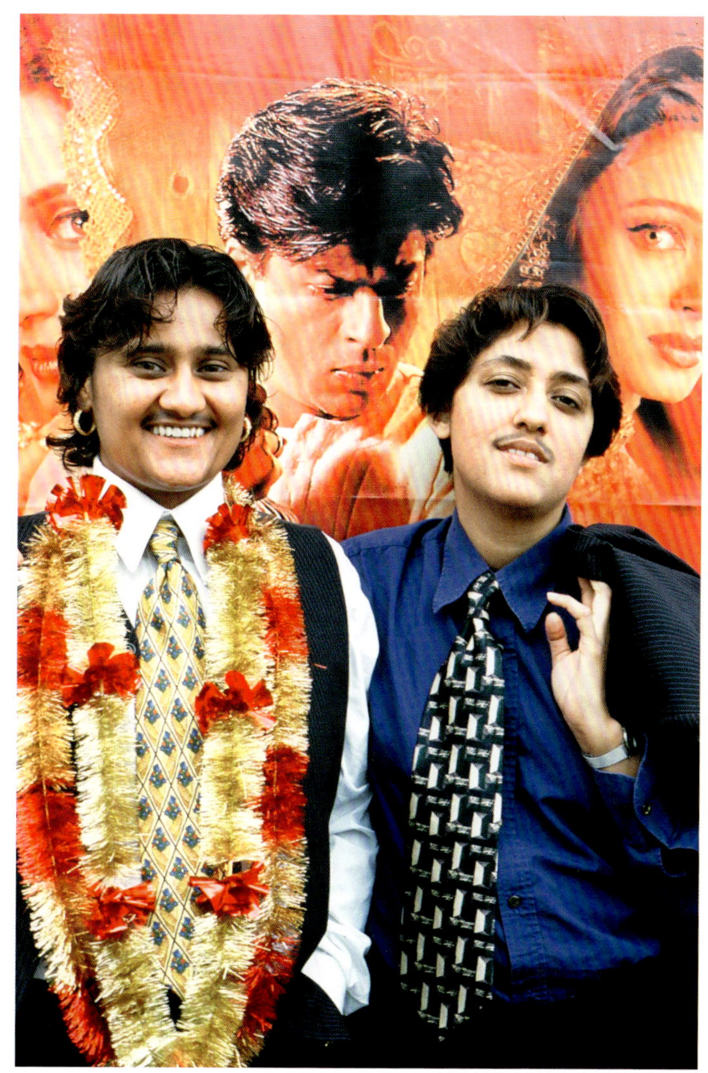

NOTES

Introduction pp.7–21

1 On the limitations of using cultural identity categories to designate artistic practices, see Diana Yeh, 'Ethnicities on the Move: "British-Chinese" Art – Identity, Subjectivity, Politics and Beyond', *Critical Quarterly*, vol.42, no.2, 2000, pp.65–91.

2 Stuart Hall, 'Black Diaspora Artists in Britain: Three "Moments" in Post-War History', *History Workshop Journal*, vol.61, no.1, 2006, pp. 1–24 (pp.2–3). On the dissensus around 'political blackness', see Valerie Mason-John and Ann Khambatta, *Making Black Waves: Lesbians Talk*, London, 1993.

3 Partition consisted of the division of British India into a self-governing, Hindu-majority India and a self-governing Muslim-majority Pakistan, encompassing the geographically separate territories of West Pakistan (now Pakistan) and East Pakistan (now Bangladesh). Partition produced the largest population movement in history, whereby at least nine million people became refugees, and at least one million people were killed in a series of massacres in the border regions.

4 Hall, 2006, p. 15.

5 Ibid., p. 5.

6 Karin Zitzewitz, 'Exodus Westwards: Padamsee, Raza and Souza in Europe', in *20th Century Indian Art: Modern, Post-Independence, Contemporary*, ed. Rakhee Balaram, Partha Mitter, and Parul Dave Mukherjee, London, 2022, pp. 172–79 (p. 174).

7 Rachel Garfield, 'Avinash Chandra: Towards a Reappraisal', in *Avinash Chandra: A Retrospective*, exh. cat., Osborne Samuel LLP and Berkeley Square Gallery, London, 2006, pp. 7–13: 9–11.

8 Rasheed Araeen (ed.), 'In the Citadel of Modernism', in *The Other Story: Afro-Asian Artists in Post-War Britain*, exh. cat., Hayward Gallery, London, 1989, pp.16–49 (pp.41–2).

9 Naseem Khan, 'Maria Souza', *Bazaar: South Asian Arts Magazine*, no.3, 1987, p. 17.

10 Art historian Partha Mitter calls this 'the Picasso manqué syndrome'. See Partha Mitter, *The Triumph of Modernism: India's Artists and the Avant-Garde, 1922–47*, London, 2007, pp. 7–10.

11 Hall, 2006, p.16.

12 Yashwant Mali quoted in Marsha Ribeiro, 'Roots of the Indian Artists' Collectives: In Their Voices', in *The Roots of the Indian Artists' Collectives*, exh. cat., Grosvenor Gallery, London, 2019.

13 On the London-based Indian modernist collectives and their exhibitions, see Alina Khakoo, '"We Shift You": Experimental Infrastructures, Race, Gender, and Unity and Difference in Britain, 1980–97', doctoral thesis, University of Cambridge, 2024. The Indian Arts Council absorbed a separate organisation founded earlier by the poet and editor M.J. Tambimuttu. Tambimuttu first arrived in London from Ceylon in 1938, following which he was active in literary circles around Soho and Fitzrovia. This is one of many linkages between the waves of postwar British South Asian art on which this book focuses, and earlier cultural crossings between South Asia and Britain.

14 Stuart Hall, Chas Critcher, Tony Jefferson, John Clark and Brian Roberts, *Policing the Crisis: Mugging, the State, and Law and Order*, London and Basingstoke, 1978.

15 Quoted in Courtney J. Martin, 'Cyclones in the Metropole: British Artists, 1968–1989', doctoral thesis, Yale University, 2010, p. 1.

16 Interview with the author, 7 November 2021.

17 Interview with the author, 4 January 2023.

18 Naseem Khan, *The Arts Britain Ignores: The Arts of Ethnic Minorities in Britain*, London, 1976, p.9. For an assessment of liberal multiculturalism from a revolutionary anti-racist standpoint, see A. Sivanandan, 'RAT and the Degradation of Black Struggle', *Race & Class*, vol.26, no.4, 1985, pp. 1–33.

19 Hall, 2006, p. 6.

20 Quoted in P. R., 'The Horizon Gallery', *Patriot Magazine*, 22 February 1987.

21 Hall, 2006, p. 1.

22 Ibid, p. 3.

23 It is not possible within the scope of this essay to list all of the individuals and projects that constitute this collective endeavour, but the works listed in the further reading section of this book are among its many outcomes.

24 Hall, 2006, p.4.

25 I have not included any artists who have said on record that they do not want to be associated with cultural identity categories.

26 Valuable for undertaking such work is Flick Allen's concept of the 'Disoeuvre': Felicity Allen, 'Creating the "Disoeuvre": Interpreting Feminist Interventions as an Expanded Artistic Practice in Negotiation with Art's Institutions', doctoral thesis, Middlesex University, 2016.

Artist Entries pp.22–149

1 Rasheed Araeen, 'Conversation With Avinash Chandra', *Third Text*, vol.2, no.3–4, 1988, pp.69–95 (p.90).

2 Gemma Sharpe, 'The Odder Story: Iqbal Geoffrey's London', unpublished paper delivered at the conference 'London, Asia, Art, Worlds', Paul Mellon Centre, London, June 2021.

3 Quoted in '*Epitaph 1958,* 1958, Iqbal Geoffrey' (catalogue entry), Tate, [n.d.], www.tate.org.uk/art/artworks/geoffrey-epitaph-1958-t00539, accessed 21 April 2025.

4 F.N. Souza, *Words and Lines*, London, 1959, p.7.

5 Gregory Salter, *Art and Masculinity in Post-War Britain: Reconstructing Home*, London, 2020, pp.121–4.

6 David Gordon White (ed.), 'Tantra in Practice: Mapping a Tradition', in *Tantra in Practice*, Princeton, 2000, pp.3–40 (p.9).

7 Prafulla Mohanti, *Through Brown Eyes*, Oxford, 1985, pp.65–99. My heartfelt thanks to Shalmali Shetty for guiding this reading.

8 Ibid.

9 Denis Bowen, introduction printed in the brochure for *Munira Al Kazi*, New Vision Centre Gallery, London, 1964, Tate Library, Main Collection, ALKAZI.

10 Hall, 2006, p.5.

11 Ibid.

12 Quoted in David Buckman, *Lancelot Ribeiro: An Artist in India and Europe*, London, 2014, pp.22–3.

13 Sukhdev Sandhu, *London Calling: How Black and Asian Writers Imagined a City*, New York, 2004, p.xxi.

14 Araeen, 1988, p.76.

15 Ronald Alley, *Catalogue of the Tate Gallery's Collection of Modern Art Other Than Works by British Artists*, London, 1981, p.117. Here, as in many of Chandra's works, women's bodies and body parts are appropriated for their aesthetic and symbolic properties, and hence dehumanised.

16 Ahmed Parvez, 'Ahmed Pervaz Writes About Himself (*Vision*, 1965)', in *Ahmed Parvez*, ed. by Marjorie Husain, Karachi, 2004, pp.10–5 (pp.13–4).

17 On the series, see Hammad Nasar, '*Meem* is for *Mashq*', in *Anwar Jalal Shemza*, ed. by Iftikhar Dadi, London, 2015, pp.181–6.

18 Interview with author, 16 August 2024.

19 Ibid.

20 Khan, 1987, p.17.

21 Rasheed Araeen, 'Preliminary Notes for a BLACK MANIFESTO', *Black Phoenix: Journal of Contemporary Art & Culture in the Third World*, no.1, 1978, pp.3–12 (p.10).

22 Namely, the armed conflict that continued between self-proclaimed Communist powers and the genocide carried out by the Khmer Rouge in Cambodia. Kylie Y. Gilchrist, 'Structures of Transformation: The Politics of Artistic Form in the Work of Rasheed Araeen, 1950s–1970s', PhD thesis, University of Manchester, 2024, p.352.

23 MPPW changed its name to the Mount Pleasant Media Workshop in the early 1990s, then to the Media Workshop, Southampton, before its closure in 2013. It was latterly run by Martin Reid.

24 'Editorial', *Step Forward*, no.11, 1988, p.2. Quoted in Christopher Pinney, 'The Event of Representation', in *Our Faces, Our Spaces: Photography, Community and Representation*, ed. by Judy Harrison, Southampton, 2013, pp.33–39 (p.33).

25 Pinney, 2013, p. 39.

26 On South Asian practices, see Syed Akbar Haider, *Reliving Karbala: Martyrdom in South Asian Memory*, Oxford, 2006.

27 Ali Nobil Ahmad, 'Between the Sacred and the Profane', 2018, recorded talk included on the re-release of *The Blood of Hussain*, dir. by Jamil Dehlavi, UK, 1980; BFI, 2018.

28 Ranajit Guha, 'The Migrant's Time', *Postcolonial Studies: Culture, Politics, Economy*, vol.1, no.2, 1998, pp.155–60 (p.156). Italics in original.

29 Cathy Wade in Cathy Wade and Yugesh Walia, 'We Were Learning on the Go: An Interview With Yugesh Walia', Vivid Projects, 19 June 2020, www.vividprojects.org.uk/wp-content/uploads/2020/07/We-were-learning-on-the-go.-An-Interview-with-Yugesh-Walia-on-the-19th-of-June-2020-by-Cathy-Wade.-.pdf, accessed 31 January 2025.

30 This conjuncture was marked by the rise of the National Front as well as police brutality and complicity in neo-fascist violence, against which the streets of British cities witnessed an outpouring of grief and rage by racialised constituencies and their comrades at the turn of the 1980s.

31 The *Riot* series was made with master printmaker Stanley Jones, who worked at the Slade School of Art's printmaking department, where Burman was a student at the time.

32 Cultural studies scholars John Benyon and John Solomos wrote that a raid on residences in Railton Road, Brixton in 1981, 'and the resultant violence on the streets of Brixton, convinced many people that the way policing is carried out is a vital factor in the context of urban unrest. An inquiry into the Railton Road raid by the Police Complaints Board discovered [...] an "institutional disregard for the niceties of the law".' John Benyon and John Solomos (ed.), 'British Urban Unrest in the 1980s', in *The Roots of Urban Unrest*, Oxford, 1987, pp.3–21 (pp.4–5).

33 See John Akomfrah, 'Black Independent Film-Making; A Statement by the Black Audio/Film Collective', *Artrage*, no.3-4, 1983, pp.29-30.

34 Reece Auguiste, 'Handsworth Songs: Some Background Notes (1988)', in *Ghosts of Songs: The Film Art of the Black Audio Film Collective*, ed. by Kodwo Eshun and Anjalika Sagar, Liverpool, 2007, pp.156-7 (p.157).

35 Kwame Ture and Charles V. Hamilton, *Black Power: The Politics of Liberation in America*, London, 1968, pp.38–47.

36 At the time, Pollock was Biswas's tutor in the Department of Fine Art at the University of Leeds, which had been transformed into the institutional base of 'social art history' since art historian T.J. Clark's appointment as Chair in 1975.

37 This included the Asian Youth Movements (AYMs), who used 'kala' in the titles of their periodicals. Biswas would have seen the AYMs' protest materials when she attended a demonstration for the Bradford 12 (on trial for preparing petrol bombs to defend themselves against civilian neo-fascist violence) in 1982. Biswas also notes that while she herself is an atheist, she was raised in a non-orthodox Bengali Hindu community in which she encountered the annual celebration of Kali, whose name and assignation in Bengali literally translates to 'black' goddess.

38 Sutapa Biswas and Courtney J. Martin, 'On *Housewives with Steak-Knives*: Sutapa Biswas in Conversation with Courtney J. Martin', in *Lumen: Sutapa Biswas*, ed. Amy Tobin, exh. cat., Ridinghouse, BALTIC Centre for Contemporary Art and Kettle's Yard, Gateshead and Cambridge, 2021, pp.23–32 (p.30).

39 Interview with the author, 16 February 2024.

40 See Bikram Narayan Nanda, *Contours of Continuity and Change: The Story of the Bonda Highlanders*, New Delhi, Thousand Oaks and London, 1994.

41 In 1982, the Association of Cinematograph, Television and Allied Technicians, in conjunction with the British Film Institute, English Regional Arts Associations, the Welsh Arts Council, and the newly inaugurated Channel 4, issued the *Grant-Aided Workshop Production Declaration*. This guaranteed ongoing financial support for 'franchised' organisations in the independent film and television sector that worked on a non-commercial, non-profit basis, as well as an outlet for their work on Channel 4.

42 NUBlockMuseum, '"A workshop focused on issues that mattered": A Conversation with Retake Film and Video Collective co-founder Ahmed Alauddin Jamal [Video]', *Stories from the Block*, 15 February 2021, www.nublockmuseum.blog/2021/02/15/a-workshop-focused-on-issues-that-mattered-a-conversation-with-retake-film-and-video-collective-co-founder-ahmed-alauddin-jamal-video/, accessed 13 January 2025.

43 Mark Crinson, 'Imperial Story-Lands: Architecture and Display at the Imperial and Commonwealth Institutes', *Art History*, vol.22, no.1, 1999, pp.99–123 (p.120).

44 Shanti Thomas, 'Journeying' [n.d.], London, Tate Library, Panchayat Ephemera: Shanti Thomas.

45   Larry D. Lutchmansingh, 'Emergent Perspectives in Modern Art: The '43 Group – Formation of a Sri Lankan Avant-Garde', in *The Sri Lanka Reader: History, Culture, Politics*, ed. John Clifford Holt, Durham, 2011, pp.574–88 (p.586).

46   Ivan Peries quoted in Senake Bandaranayake and Manel Fonseka, *Ivan Peries: Paintings 1938–88*, Colombo, 1996, p.43.

47   Poulomi Desai and Sunil Gupta, 'Breaking Boundaries: Poulomi Desai in Conversation with Sunil Gupta', in *Red Threads: The South Asian Queer Connection in Photographs*, ed. by Poulomi Desai and Parminder Sekhon, London, 2003, pp.55–8 (p.55).

48   Maud Sulter, statement printed on the brochure for *Check It!*, a festival at the Drill Hall Arts Centre, London, 1985. Quoted in Maud Sulter (ed.), 'Blackwomen's Creativity Project: An Overview', in *Passion: Discourses on Blackwomen's Creativity*, Hebden Bridge, 1990, pp.15–18 (p.17).

49   Ruhul Amin and Sarita Malik, 'Let's Not Talk About It: Sarita Malik Interviews Bengali Filmmaker Ruhul Amin', *Black Film Bulletin*, vol.2, no.3, 1994, pp.20–1 (p.21).

50   Ibid., p.20.

51   As described in Brian McAvera, *Avtarjeet Dhanjal*, London, 1997, p.64. Not all these elements have survived. McAvera states that the title *Dunstall Henge* was coined by a local historian, while contemporary newspaper reports state that it was coined by the artist.

52   Dhanjal quoted in McAvera, 1997, p.40.

53   Nguyen demonstrates this by analysing the scene in which discussion of Omar's racist trauma perpetrated by Johnny and his friends is intertwined with the pair having sex. Gayatri Chakravorty Spivak, *Outside in the Teaching Machine*, New York, 2012, p.280; Vinh Nguyen, 'Queer Intimacy and the Impasse: Reconsidering *My Beautiful Laundrette*', *Ariel: A Review of International English Literature*, vol.48, no.2, 2017, pp.155–66 (pp.155, 161–3).

54   Lubaina Himid (ed.), 'Letters to Susan', in *Thin Black Line(s)*, Preston, 2011, pp.7–26 (p.12).

55   Mahmood Mamdani, *Neither Settler nor Native: The Making and Unmaking of Permanent Minorities*, Cambridge, 2020, pp.344–52.

56   Interview with the author, 28 July 2024.

57   The installation consists of four double-sided panels that are suspended from the ceiling, with chilli and turmeric powders scattered on the floor beneath.

58   The poem reads, 'EACH MORNING AT 5:00a.m. THEY SCRUBBED THE FLOOR – SOME ONE | OFFERED HER A DAY'S WORK. SOMETIMES THESE WHITE PEOPLE ON THE WAY TO WORK LAUGHED AT THEIR INDIANNESS . . . | SHOUTED PAKI: AAPRI BHENO. | SUCKED THEIR TEETH, DISMISSING THEM. . .'. 'Aapri bheno' means 'our sisters' in Gujarati.

59   Mark Haworth-Booth, 'Zarina Bhimji', *British Journal of Photography*, 24 March 1994, p.17. In the 1970s, numerous South Asian women were subjected to gynaecological examinations by immigration staff in Britain and its High Commissions in South Asia. Suspecting abuse of the 1971 Immigration Act, which fast-tracked fiancées of migrant workers into Britain, officers sought physical proof that these women were unmarried, childless and therefore virgins.

60   Allison K. Young, 'Lady of Silences: The Enigmatic Photo-Text Work of Zarina Bhimji', *British Art Studies*, no.20, 2021.

61   Priya Mookerjee, *Pathway Icons: The Wayside Art of India*, London, 1987, p.12.

62   Sonali Fernando, 'The Artists', in *Transition of Riches*, exh. cat., Birmingham City Museum and Art Gallery, Birmingham, 1993, pp.17–49 (p.36).

63   Edward W. Said, 'Reflections on Exile', in *Reflections on Exile: and Other Literary and Cultural Essays*, 2nd edn, London, 2012, pp.173–86 (p.179).

64   Following the incremental implementation of policies aimed at disenfranchising Uganda's privileged South Asian population, Idi Amin, who had seized the presidency in a coup in 1971, issued an expulsion order in August 1972. The majority, an estimated 25,000 people, fled to Britain.

65   Chris Mullard quoted in Yasmin Alibhai, 'Community whitewash', *Guardian*, 23 January 1989.

66   Hamad Butt, 'Apprehensions', in *Familiars*, ed. by Stephen Foster and Gilane Tawadros, London,

1996, pp.35–54.

67   Yong Soon Min describes that there was handwritten text inscribed onto the two bodies, and that the artwork comprised multiple panels and had a semi-transparent veil. Yong Soon Min, 'Al-An deSouza', in *Crossing Black Waters*, exh. cat. City Gallery, Leicester, 1992, pp.26–9.

68   Salman Rushdie, *The Satanic Verses*, London, 1998, p. 7.

69   Yong Soon Min, 1992, p.29.

70   Kellie Jones, 'In Their Own Image', *Artforum*, vol.29, no.3, 1990, pp.132–8 (p.134).

71   Stuart Hall, 'Black Narcissus' (excerpt), *Autograph: The Association of Black Photographers Newsletter*, June 1991, pp.1–2 (p.2).

72   Frederic Leighton's Holland Park home, a collaboration with George Aitchison, William De Morgan and Walter Crane, built between 1877 and 1879, is one of London's most famous nineteenth-century Orientalist interiors.

73   Deborah Swallow, 'Shanti Panchal: An Introduction', in *Shanti Panchal: A Personal Journey*, exh. cat., British Council, Mumbai, 2003, pp.1–2 (p.1).

74   Shanti Panchal in Shanti Panchal and Philip Vann, 'Shanti Panchal: Intuitive Power', *The Artist's and Illustrator's Magazine*, no.43, 1990, pp.20–23 (pp.20–22).

75   Carol Mavor, *Reading Boyishly: Roland Barthes, J. M. Barrie, Jacques Henri Lartigue, Marcel Proust, and D. W. Winnicott*, Durham, 2007, p.135.

76   Gill Park, 'The Pavilion Women's Photography Center 1983–1993: Deciphering an "Incomplete" [Feminist] Project', PhD thesis, University of Leeds, 2018, p.263.

77   Sharma writes, 'My parents' store near Reading was the perfect place to learn about society as a child, absorbing shoppers' thoughts and habits . . . Customers would regularly dissect newspaper headlines with Mum and Dad in a way that would give prime minister's questions a run for its money.' Babita Sharma, 'Counter Culture: My Life Growing Up in a Corner Shop', *Guardian*, 19 May 2019, www.theguardian.com/society/2019/may/19/counter-culture-my-life-growing-up-in-a-corner-shop-babita-sharma, accessed 30 January 2025. Afza's corner shop, with a white customer depicted in the background, and an Urdu notice displayed behind the counter, is indeed a site of everyday encounter with social difference.

78   Keith Khan, 'A Celebration of Carnival', [1988], London, Goldsmiths University Special Collections, FH/MR/KK/002.

79   An initial title for *Apple Green* was *Lake in January*, referring to the work's inspiration: a pond on London's Hampstead Heath.

80   Araeen, 1989, p.44; Kaushalia Khanna, 'A Mystery at Play', *Tate Etc.*, 3 September 2024, www.tate.org.uk/tate-etc/issue-62-summer-2024/a-mystery-at-play, accessed 31 January 2025.

81   Rushdie, 1998, p.5.

82   Sonali Fernando includes other elements in her account of the work: Sonali Fernando, 'Scaffolding of the Bone House: An Interview with Installation Artist Alistair Raphael', *Rungh*, vol.1, no.4, 1993, pp.16-8. However, I could not corroborate this with documentation in the Camerawork archive or contemporary reviews.

83   Alistair Raphael quoted in Fernando, 1993, p.16; Roberto Esposito, *Immunitas: The Protection and Negation of Life*, trans. by Zakiya Hanafi, Cambridge, 2011.

84   Maud Sulter (ed.), 'Empowerment', in *Passion: Discourses on Blackwomen's Creativity*, Hebden Bridge, 1990, pp.249–54 (p.249).

85   Photocopy of Harriet Gaze and Samena Rana, 'Camera Woman', *LINK*, 1991, London, Tate Library, Panchayat Ephemera: Samena Rana.

86   Lisa Tickner, *Hornsey 1968: The Art School Revolution*, London, 2008.

87   Interview with the author, 30 September 2024.

88   Kikoi is a rectangular-shaped, woven cotton textile; kitenge is a wax-printed textile.

89   Interview with the author, 30 September 2024.

90   Gargi Bhattacharyya and John Gabriel, 'Gurinder Chadha and the Apna Generation: Black British Film in the 1990s', *Third Text*, vol.8, no.27, 1994, pp.55–63 (pp.60–61).

91   See *Panjabis of Southall: 70 Years of Struggles and Achievements*, dir. by The Asian Health Agency, digital- works, 2019, www.digital-works.co.uk/

southall.html, accessed 21 April 2025.

92 Bhattacharyya and Gabriel, 1994, p.57.

93 Alina Khakoo, 'Staying with the Ambivalence: An Interview with Permindar Kaur', Art UK, 26 February 2025, www.artuk.org/discover/stories/staying-with-the-ambivalence-an-interview-with-permindar-kaur, accessed 21 April 2025.

94 From left to right in this photograph, the activists symbolised were: Annie Besant, Sarojini Naidu, Bina Das, Kamala Nehru, Rani Jhansi Lakshmi Bai and Begum Jahan Ara Shah Nawaz.

95 See Alice Correia, 'Diasporic Returns: Reading Partition in Contemporary Art', *Third Text*, vol.31, no.2–3, 2017, pp.321–40.

96 See Veena Das, *Life and Words: Violence and the Descent into the Ordinary*, Berkeley, Los Angeles and London, 2007.

97 Quoted in 'Juginder Lamba', South Asian Diaspora Arts Archive [n.d.], www.sadaa.co.uk/studio/files/Jaginda-Lamba_biog.pdf, accessed 31 January 2025.

98 Juginder Lamba quoted in Celeste-Marie Bernier, *Stick to the Skin: African American and Black British Art, 1965–2015*, Berkeley, 2018, p.73.

99 'Juginder Lamba'. Makonde sculpture, comprising intricate patterns carved on African blackwood, emerged in Mozambique in the late colonial period, prompted by the patronage of missionaries and traders, and was largely produced for an export market.

100 Jacqueline Rose, *Mothers: An Essay on Love and Cruelty*, 2nd edn, London, 2019, p.15.

101 Jai Chuhan, Artist's Statement, in *Transition of Riches*, p.54.

102 Indeed, this was a moment when many of Chuhan's contemporaries in feminist, anti-racist cultural activist circles had stopped practising, as they entered into their thirties and prioritised caring responsibilities for children and ageing parents. See Janice Cheddie, Simone Alexander and Symrath Patti, 'You Can't Eat Prestige: Women, Reinvention and the Archival Trace: Conversation Between Janice Cheddie, Simone Alexander and Symrath Patti', Panchayat Collection Research Resource, Tate Library, www.tate.org.uk/research/panchayat-collection-research-resource/you-cant-eat-prestige-women-reinvention-and-the-archival-trace, accessed 31 January 2025.

103 *The Satanic Verses* 1988 was seen by many Muslims as an attack on their faith, and as perpetuating colonial stereotypes of Islam. The British media took little interest in peaceful protests against the publication, but the burning of a copy of the book in Bradford was sensationalised, leading to a public outpouring of racist attitudes and a rise in racist attacks, including three murders in the summer of 1989. Tensions were heightened by Ayatollah Khomeini's fatwa.

104 Sarbjit Natt, Artist's Statement, in *Transition of Riches*, p.50.

105 The Indo-Fijian diaspora is a double diaspora, which first experienced displacement as indentured labourers brought from India to Fiji under British colonial rule, to work on sugar plantations in the late-nineteenth to early-twentieth centuries, following which a well-established, successful, fourth generation left Fiji in the face of racial and economic pressures that followed a military coup in 1987.

106 Gayatri Gopinath, *Impossible Desires: Queer Diasporas and South Asian Public Cultures*, Durham, 2005, p.68. Gopinath also points out that this is made possible by the absence of the diasporic feminine subject, namely Amin's mother, who, the viewer is told, is at the mosque during the film shoot.

107 Emma Wilson, *Love, Mortality and the Moving Image*, Basingstoke, 2012, p.14.

108 Interview with the author, 29 August 2024.

109 Quoted in 'Syed Saleem Arif Quadri MBE', South Asian Diaspora Arts Archive [n.d.], www.sadaa.co.uk/studio/files/Saleem-Arif-Quadri_biog-1.pdf, accessed 31 January 2025.

110 Imogen Cornwall-Jones, '*Landscape of Longing*, 1997-9, Saleem Arif Quadri' (collection text), Tate, 2001, www.tate.org.uk/art/artworks/quadri-landscape-of-longing-t07710, accessed 21 April 2025; Hassan Vawda, 'Faith, Heritage and Negative Space: An Interview with Saleem Arif Quadri', Art

UK, 24 February 2025, www.artuk.org/discover/
stories/faith-heritage-and-negative-space-an-
interview-with-saleem-arif-quadri/sort_by/
publication_date/order/desc/page/1/view_as/grid,
accessed 21 April 2025.

111   Cherry Smyth, 'Out of the Gaps: The Work of
Parminder Sekhon', in *Red Threads*, pp.103–10
(p.110).

112   Smyth, 2003, p.104.

FURTHER READING

Publications

Aikens, Nick, and Elizabeth Robles, eds., *The Place Is Here: The Work of Black Artists in 1980s Britain*, Berlin and Eindhoven, 2019

Araeen, Rasheed, ed., *The Other Story: Afro-Asian Artists in Post-War Britain*, exh. cat., Hayward Gallery, London 1989

Bailey, David A., and Stuart Hall eds., *Critical Decade: Black British Photography in the 80s*, special issue of *Ten.8*, 2.3 (1992)

Bailey, David A., Ian Baucom, and Sonia Boyce, eds., *Shades of Black: Assembling Black Arts in 1980s Britain*, Durham, NC and London 2005

Boyce, Sonia, and Dorothy Price, eds., *Rethinking British Art: Black Artists and Modernism*, special issue of *Art History*, 44.3 (2021)

Brah, Avtar, *Cartographies of Diaspora: Contesting Identities*, London and New York 1996

Chambers, Eddie, *Black Artists in British Art: A History Since the 1950s*, London and New York 2014

Correia, Alice, ed., *What is Black Art?: Writings on African, Asian and Caribbean Art in Britain, 1981-1989*, London 2022

Ghosh, Amal, and Juginder Lamba, eds., *Beyond Frontiers: Contemporary British Art by Artists of South Asian Descent*, London 2001

Gregory, Joy, ed., *Shining Lights: Black Women Photographers in 1980s-90s Britain*, London 2024

Mahn, Churnjeet, Rohit K. Dasgupta, and DJ Ritu, *Desi Queers: LGBTQ+ South Asians and Cultural Belonging in Britain*, London 2025

Mercer, Kobena, *Welcome to the Jungle: New Positions in Black Cultural Studies*, New York and London 1994

Mercer, Kobena, ed., *Annotating Art's Histories* series, Cambridge, MA and London 2005-8

Mercer, Kobena, ed., *Black Film British Cinema*, London 1988: www.issuu.com/icalondon/docs/ blackfilmbritishcinema, accessed 2 October 2023

Nasar, Hammad, and Sarah Victoria Turner, eds., *London, Asia, Exhibitions, Histories*, special issue of *British Art Studies*, 1.13 (2019) – see especially Alice Correia, 'Researching Exhibitions of South Asian Women Artists in Britain in the 1980s'

Nwonka, Clive, and Anamik Saha, eds., *Black Film British Cinema II*, London 2021

Sulter, Maud, ed., *Passion: Discourses on Blackwomen's Creativity*, Hebden Bridge 1990

Tharani, Nadir, ed., *Representations of South Asian Arts in Britain*, special issue of *Artrage*, 17 (1987)

Archives and digital resources

African-Caribbean, Asian and African Art in Britain Archive, Chelsea College of Arts, University of the Arts London

Ahmed Iqbal Ullah Race Relations Resource Centre, Manchester Central Library

BFI Player, South Asian Britain on Film, www.player.bfi. org.uk/free/collection/south-asian-britain-on-film

Making Britain, www.open.ac.uk/makingbritain

Panchayat Collection, Tate Library, London – see also Panchayat Collection Research Resource, www. tate.org.uk/research/panchayat-collection-research-resource

South Asian Diaspora Arts Archive, Birmingham Museum and Art Gallery – see also www.sadaa. co.uk/archive/art

Stuart Hall Library, Institute of International Visual Arts (iniva), London

Women's Art Library, Goldsmiths, University of London

COPYRIGHT AND IMAGE CREDITS

The publishers have made every effort to trace the copyright holders of the works illustrated and apologise for any omissions or errors that may have been made.

Image credits

All images are *courtesy the artist* unless otherwise stated below:

Rose Akeroyd/Art UK p.77

Courtesy the artist and Autograph, London p.141 (top)

Courtesy the artist and Birmingham Film & Video Workshop p.51

Courtesy the artist/Fukuoka Asian Art Museum p.129

Courtesy the artist (shantipanchal.com) p.105

Courtesy the artist, Tandana Archive, and the Research Centre for Global Education, Coventry University p.14

© Arts Council Collection/Bridgeman Images p.111

Arts Council Collection, Southbank Centre, London pp.67, 127, 137

Courtesy the BFI National Archive pp.63, 75, 123 (both)

Bradford District Museums & Galleries CBMDC pp.93, 119, 131, 139, 145

© Bradford Museums & Galleries/Bridgeman Images pp.49, 95

Courtesy Christie's p.41

DACS Images p.85

DACS Images. Photo: Andy Keates front cover, p.59

DACS Images. Courtesy Lisson Gallery and Smoking Dogs Films p.55

Graham Lester George, courtesy the Estate of Gurminder Sikand p.121

Courtesy the Government Museum and Art Gallery, Chandigarh, India p.23

Courtesy Judy Panesar Harrison p.45

Courtesy The Hepworth Wakefield p.29

Manchester Art Gallery/Bridgeman Images p.37

Courtesy The Otolith Group p.19

Swen Paterson, courtesy the artist p.115

Edward Prosser p.141 (bottom)

Courtesy the Estate of Samena Rana p.117

Courtesy the Estate of F N Souza p.9

© Tate back cover, pp.16 (both), 25, 27, 33, 34-5, 39, 43, 53, 79, 97, 147

© Victoria and Albert Museum, London pp.31, 69

Copyright credits

All works are © *the artist* unless otherwise stated below:

© Estate of Munira Al-Kazi p.31

© Rasheed Araeen. All Rights Reserved, DACS 2025 p.43

© Zarina Bhimji. All Rights Reserved, DACS 2025 pp.16 (right), 85

© Sutapa Biswas. All Rights Reserved, DACS 2025 front cover, p.59

© Chila Kumari Singh Burman. All Rights Reserved, DACS 2025 p.53

© Jamal Butt p.97

© Estate of Avinash Chandra pp.34-5

© Mohini Chandra/Autograph p.141

© Estate of Avtarjeet Singh Dhanjal p.77

© Nina Edge. All Rights Reserved, DACS 2025 pp.16 (left), 73

© Estate of Iqbal Geoffrey p.25

© Estate of Amal Ghosh p.93

© Government Museum & Art Gallery, Chandigarh. Acknowledgement for information provided and verified by Alita Chandra, the daughter of Prem Lata Chandra p.23

© Sunil Gupta. All Rights Reserved, DACS 2025 p.79

© Judy Panesar Harrison p.45

© Permindar Kaur. All Rights Reserved, DACS 2025 p.127

© Balraj Khanna. All Rights Reserved, DACS 2025 p.111

© The Otolith Group p.19

© Estate of Ahmed Parvez p.37

© Estate of Ivan Peries p.69

© Estate of Samena Rana (keeper Shaheen Merali) p.117

© Retake Film and Video Collective p.63

© Estate of Lancelot Ribeiro. All Rights Reserved. DACS 2025 p.33

© Estate of Anwar Jalal Shemza. All Rights Reserved, DACS 2025 back cover, p.39

© Estate of Gurminder Sikand p.121

© Smoking Dogs Films, All Rights Reserved, DACS 2025 p.55

© Estate of F. N. Souza. All Rights Reserved, DACS 2025 p.27

© Estate of Maria Souza p.41

INDEX

'43 Group 68

Academy of Fine Art, Florence 66
Adrus, Said 12, 94, 120
    Portrait of Another Kind 94, 95
Afza, Nudrat 12, 106
    Shop, Gibbet Street 106, 107
Ahmad, Ali Nobil 46
Ahmed, Fatima 8, 134
    Untitled 134, 135
AIDS epidemic 96, 112
Akmut, Nilofar 12, 128
    Dear Women of the Indian Subcontinent 128, 129
Al Kazi, Munira 8, 11, 30
    Mother 30, 31
Amin, Ruhul 12, 74
    A Kind of English 74, 75
anti-racist movements 8, 13, 14, *14*, 15, 26, 42, 50, 52, 54, 58,
    60, 62, 80, 82, 90, 98, 108, 114, 122, 132, 142
Araeen, Rasheed 8, 10, 12, 18, 42, 62, 110
    Fire! 12, 42, 43
Artists for Democracy 12, 42
Arts 38, London 11, 26, 40, 134
Asian Artists' Group (AAG) 120
Autograph (organisation) 70, 100

Batra, Raj 56
Bhimji, Zarina 12, 15, 84
    She Loved to Breathe – Pure Silence 15, 16, 84, 85
Birmingham Film and Video Workshop 50
Birmingham School of Photography 50
Biswas, Sutapa 12, 15, 58, 120
    Housewives With Steak-Knives 58, 59, 80
Black Audio Film Collective 12, 19, 54
    Expeditions 1 – Signs of Empire 54, 55
    O Horizon 19, 19
Blackwomen's Creativity Project 15–16, 72, 114
Bluecoat, Liverpool, *A Table for Four* (exh., 1991) 114
British Black Arts Movement 52, 70, 80, 90, 116, 120, 126
British Empire *see* colonialism
British South Asian postwar art
    first wave 8–12, 20–1
    second wave 8, 12–21
Britishness 7, 94

Brixton Art Gallery 66
Burman, Chila Kumari Singh 12, 52, 124
    Cut - Foot - Pupil - Uprisings 52, 53
Butt, Hamad 12, 96
    Transmission 96, 97

Camerawork, London, *Darshan* (exh., 1986) 60
capitalism 28, 76, 90
Caravaggio 66
caste system 15, 132
Chadha, Gurinder 12, 122
    Bhaji on the Beach 122, 123
Chandra, Avinash 8, 10, 11, 32, 34, 36, 38
    Hills of Gold 11, 34, 34–5
Chandra, Mohini 12, 140
    album pacifica 1 140, 141
Chandra, Prem Lata 8, 22, 134
    Untitled 22, 23
Chuhan, Jai 12, 136
    Self Portrait 136, 137
College of Fine Arts, Hyderabad 134
colonialism 8, 10, 13, 26, 32, 38, 68, 90, 96, 98, 102, 108, 130,
    140; *see also* decolonisation; postcolonialism
Commonwealth Institute, London 11, 64

Das, Prodeepta 18, 60
    Bonda Women, Malkangiri, from the series The Hill
      of Flutes: Images of Odisha 60, 61
decolonisation 8–10, 11, 16, 19, 128
Dehlavi, Jamil 12, 46, 108
    The Blood of Hussain 46, 47
Delhi Polytechnic 22
Desai, Poulomi 12, 70
    In the Box Room 70, 71
deSouza, Al-An 12, 15, 16, 98
    Spit and Polish 98, 99
Dhanjal, Avtarjeet Singh 18, 76
    Dunstall Henge 76, 77
Digwa, Sucha Singh, *Untitled 44, 45*
Disability Arts Movement 116
Dodd, Stephen 78, *79*

Edge, Nina 12, 72, 120
    Snakes and Ladders 15, 72, 73

Fanon, Frantz, *Black Skin, White Masks* 56

feminism 7, 15, 58, 66, 72, 80, 82, 84, 88, 100, 114, 116, 120,
    122, 124, 128, 132, 134
Format (agency) 100

Gallery One, London 11
gender 15, 58, 70, 72, 84, 98, 102, 134, 142
Gentileschi, Artemisia 58
Geoffrey, Iqbal 8, 24
    Epitaph 24, 25
geometric abstraction 22, 24, 38
Ghosh, Amal 8, 92
    Flight II 92, 93
Gill, Sardul 18, 19, 86, 120
    Earth Shrine 86, 87
Goldsmith's College, London 96
Gombrich, Ernst 38
Government Museum and Art Gallery, Chandigarh 22
Gupta, Sunil 12, 70, 78
    Gay from the series *Reflections of the Black
    Experience 78, 79*

Hall, Stuart 8–9, 11, 19, 20, 30, 32
Harrison, Judy 15, 44
Hatoum, Mona, *Under Siege* 80
Himid, Lubaina 80
Hinduism 130, 138
Horizon Gallery, London 17, *18*, 40
Hunjan, Bhajan 18, 124
    Dialogue II 6, 124, 125

IAUK Gallery, London, *Four Indian Women Artists* (exh.,
    1981–2) 124
Imperial War Museum, London 104
India House, *Six Indian Painters* (exh., 1964) 12
Indian Arts Council 12, 17
Indian Painters' Collective 11
Indian Women's Movement 134
international modernism 22, 26, 32, 38, 68
Islamic art and culture 30, 38, 84, 102

Karimjee, Mumtaz 12, 88
    In Search of an Image 88, 89, 102
Kathakali dance 114
Kaur, Permindar 12, 126
    Innocence 126, 127
Kempadoo, Roshini 12, 100

Identity in Production 70, 100, 101
Khan, Keith 12, 108, 144
    Flying Costumes, Floating Tombs 108, 109
Khan, Naseem, *The Art Britain Ignores* (report) 17
Khanna, Balraj 8, 10, 17, 19, 110, 146
    Apple Green 110, 111
Kureishi, Hanif, and Stephen Frears, *My Beautiful
    Laundrette 78*

Lamba, Juginder 18, 130
    Lovers 130, 131

Maan, Shakila Taranum 12, 102
    Ferdous 102, 103
Madhubani art 120
Mahapatra, Sitakant 60
Mali, Yashwant 11
Matisse, Henri 146
McKenzie, Anita J. 12, 132
    *Mother and Daughter from the series Imaging The
    Black Family 132, 133*
Meiling Jin 80
Merali, Shaheen 12, 90
    Unilever Strike 90, 91
Middlesex Polytechnic 118
Mohanti, Prafulla 8, 28
    Composition 28, 29
Mount Pleasant Photography Workshop (MPPW) 12,
    15, 44
    Untitled 44, 45
Mughal art and culture 138
Mukti magazine 15, *16*

Natt, Sarbjit 12, 138
    Mughal 118, 138, 139
Naz (organisation) 15
neo-tantrism 28
New Vision Centre, London 11, 30

Orientalism 88, 102
The Otolith Group, *O Horizon 19, 19*

Panchal, Shanti 18, 104
    Mannequin 104, 105
Parker, Roszika 58
Parmar, Pratibha 7, 12, 70, 80

Emergence 7, 80, 81
Parvez, Ahmed 8, 36
   Waiting for the Cloud 36, 37
Passion: Discourses on Blackwomen's Creativity
   (anthology) 15, 16, 114
Patti, Symrath 12, 56
   Black Skin White Masks 56, 57
People's Gallery, London 72
Peries, Ivan 8, 68
   Monk on the Seashore at Dehiwala 68, 69
Pollard, Ingrid 15
Pollock, Griselda 58
postcolonialism 10, 19, 20, 22, 24, 34, 64, 94, 98, 108, 130,
   140

Quadri, Saleem Arif 18, 146
   Landscape of Longing 146, 147
queerness 15, 70, 78, 96, 102, 112, 142, 144, 148
Qureshi, Fahim 14
   Photograph of picket in Luton 14

Racism 10, 13, 15, 26, 28, 34, 42, 44, 50, 52, 54, 56, 58, 60,
   62, 72, 74, 80, 82, 84, 116, 132, 142; *see also* anti-racism
   movements
Rainbow Art Group 12
Rana, Samena 12, 15, 116
   Desk from the series Bottom Drawer 116, 117
Raphael, Alistair 12, 112
   Invasive Procedures 112, 113
Rashid, Ian Iqbal 12, 16-17, 142
   Surviving Sabu 142, 143
Retake Film and Video Collective 12, 62
   Majdhar 62, 63
Ribeiro, Lancelot 8, 32, 36, 134
   Cityscape (Night) 32, 33
Rushdie, Salman, *The Satanic Verses* 98, 102, 110

Sahara (women's refuge) 124
Said, Edward 94
Sandhu, Sukhdev 32
Sekhon, Parminder 12, 15, 70, 148
   Wedding Guests of the Bride 148, 149
Shah, Fahmida 12, 118
   Untitled 118, 119
Shemza, Anwar Jalal 8, 38
   Meem Two 38, 39
Shinhat, Molly 12, 82

I'm the problem, I'm not white 82, 83
Sikand, Gurminder 12, 120
   Enclosure 120, 121
Sikhism 126, 138
Sir John Cass School of Art, London 116
Slade School of Fine Art, London 38
Southall Youth Movement 70
Southampton Photographic Gallery 44
Souza, F.N. 8, 9, 10, 11, 26, 38, 40, 134
   Crucifixion 26, 27
   'Nirvana of a Maggot' 26
Souza, Maria 8, 11, 26, 40
   Possibly a sketch for a silk velvet dress with Rajasthani
     mirror embellishment 40, 41
Spender, Stephen 26
Stephen Lawrence Gallery, University of Greenwich 132
Stephenson, Veena 12, 114
   Looking for Clues … Finding Them 114, 115
Sulter, Maud 15, 72, 114

Tagore, Rabindranath 19
Tate Gallery 11
Tharani, Nadir 18, 64
   Structure for the Commonwealth Institute's African
     Music Village, Holland Park, London 64, 65
Thomas, Shanti 18, 66
   The Voyagers 66, 67

Uddin, Shafique 12, 48
   Relatives Gather at the Dead Woman's House; She
     Became Ill and Died Suddenly 48, 49

Walia, Sunandan and Yugesh 12, 15, 50
   Mirror, Mirror 50, 51
   Shadows of Caste 15
Walker, Alice 114
Windrush Generation 13
Women Against Fundamentalism (WAF, group) 102
Women's Liberation Movement 58, 134
Women's Work Collective 66
Wyndham, John, *The Day of the Triffids* 96

Yong Soon Min 98

Zaidi, Ali Mehdi 12, 144
   Of Fears and Desires 144, 145